Young adult offenders and crime policy

proceedings

**Reports presented to the
10th Criminological Colloquy (1991)**

European Committee on Crime Problems

Criminological research, Vol. XXX

Council of Europe Press, 1994

French edition:

Jeunes adultes délinquants et politique criminelle

ISBN 92-871-2183-4

Publishing and Documentation Service
Council of Europe
F-67075 Strasbourg Cedex

ISBN 92-871-2184-2
© Council of Europe, 1994
Printed in the Netherlands

CONTENTS

Page

Contents

YOUNG ADULT OFFENDERS AND CRIME POLICY

INTRODUCTORY REPORT

by
Mrs V. Lenoir-Degoumois,
General Rapporteur, Professor Emeritus,
University of Lausanne (Switzerland)

INTRODUCTION

To celebrate its 10th Criminological Colloquium, the Council of Europe has chosen a fascinating and difficult theme which will appeal to any contemporary criminologist as it concerns young adult offenders - who have the highest statistical crime rate - and the pertinent crime policy. The replies here to the questions discussed will perhaps give a new bias to many European systems.

The colloquium has the privilege of including representatives from the countries of eastern Europe; throughout the profound events they are experiencing they are facing fundamental problems in crime policy which they will share with their western colleagues while taking a new and critical look at the experiences of the west.

We shall be advocating guidelines - in the form of recommendations - which may be followed by all member states of the Council of Europe. We shall be trying to envisage not a two-tier Europe but rather a fertile ground for the comparison of experiences and the development of research co-ordinated on a European scale in countries that are all motivated by a feeling of true solidarity.

1. YOUNG ADULT OFFENDERS

1.1.   All young adults - offenders or not - have certain psychological and social characteristics which must be emphasised as we begin our work.

1.1.1 Studies in development psychology show that young people do not become mature adults from one day to the next but go through intermediate phases of varying length and type. They are still close to childhood, shaking off the vestiges of adolescence, and occasionally retain for a long time immature traits which make them unsure of their identity, and easily influenced.

However, their very youth means that they are able to modify their behaviour and set off in new directions which will determine for their future; these will be positive if the young adults become convinced that they are respected as people in themselves, that they are accepted in their moments of doubt and anxiety and that they are encouraged to take personal and moral responsibility as well as exercising self-control.

Hence their own interests and those of society justify efforts and sacrifices to help them live through the difficult period between the physical and psychological changes of adolescence and the age of maturity.

1.1.2. The lives of young adults are marked by relatively recent social changes. Becoming an adult is not an event depending on rites of passage such as the end of an apprenticeship, military service or marriage. On the contrary, in our modern societies, becoming adult often means starting on a latent period, of variable length, differing w idely according to whether the young adult is already financially independent or still studying, whether he lives with his parents or has his own home, whether or not he has periods of unemployment and has to rely on himself.

Whereas traditionally young adults moved from school and family control to new work and personal relationships which made them adult, today they shake off the former controls without being subject to the latter. It is a fact that this socially latent period exposes them to risks of deviation and delinquency which are all the more tempting because their current conditions are disagreeable and even hopeless.

1.1.3. We define young adults as all persons who are at that intermediate stage of psychological development and passing through that latent social period. The length of this period is currently changing because people are extending their studies and starting work later, largely because of unemployment. These young people form a real juvenile sub-culture in many countries.

This age group varies between 16 to 18 years and 21 to 23 years - sometimes up to 25 years in different places and cultures and can only be determined in an empirical way.

1.2. This largely accounts for crime among young adults.

1.2.1. In fact, statistical data show that while delinquency has greatly increased in western countries since the second world war, the increase is essentially in the young adult age group. Undoubtedly, generalisations must immediately be broken down by taking into account factors such as demography, information sources on criminal activities, the definition of delinquency (for example, drugs), rules of procedure (principle of legality and opportunity), etc.

1.2.2. Although we have examined the composition of the young adult age group in terms of psychological and sociological factors, we must pay particular attention to the causes of their criminality by examining features such as sex, socio-economic conditions, housing, the family and social background, and first and second generation immigration. Interaction of these factors undoubtedly creates a breeding ground for delinquency in some young adults.

1.2.3. The problem of recidivism in this age group also warrants serious study in that it presents characteristics which enable preventive and repressive measures to be established as part of an effective crime policy.

2. CRIME POLICY WITH REGARD TO YOUNG ADULT OFFENDERS

2.1. While appearing unremarkable, the concept of crime policy is vague, and includes all the interpretations given to it by different people, which vary according to their culture. At the outset, it is therefore necessary to give it a definition and we would propose the following: crime policy is all the procedures by which society organises responses to the occurence of crime.[1] This is one feature of the policy of a country, region or local community; from there on it will depend on the more general context in which it is placed and the <u>values</u> recognised by a given society.

Since Europe lives - or tries to live - under the rule of democracy, it is on the values of democracy which any crime policy should rely. We know them: they are laid down in the Declaration on Human Rights and, for young people under 18 years old, the recent Convention on the Rights of the Child.

2.3. In democratic systems, <u>the opinion of the people</u> plays an important role in the choice of crime policy. Now, public opinion is easily swayed by the feeling of insecurity produced by delinquency, particularly when it is expressed in demonstrations by angry young people to which the media readily gives cover ; the result is often a demand for subjective punishment requiring more severe responses to crime. So people's opinions must be forged by criminologists to combat reactions of fear, explain the selection of crime policies, make clear the issues, cost and benefits of such options and encourage voluntary co-operation by local communities in prevention and treatment measures for young adults in difficulty. That is of paramount importance at a time when criminology is at the centre of contradictory currents and is torn between preventive/curative approaches and the neo-classical alternatives advocating the need for just desserts and neutralisation.

2.4. At present, crime policy with regard to young adults in a number of countries shows great diversity with fluctuation between three main lines:

— there is a tendency to group them - at least partly - with minors and allow them to benefit from more flexible law and special jurisdiction;

— they are considered as adult criminals judged by ordinary courts and subject - with some alleviation - to the same sanctions as adults;

— or else they are given specific treatment.

An option is essential and undoubtedly considerable time will be devoted to it although there is no point in choosing it from the outset.

2.5 Whatever the system adopted, young adult offenders should be subject to <u>rules of procedure</u> safeguarding their fundamental rights and ensuring rapid intervention by the competent authorities so that the cause and effect relationship between the offence and society's reaction is clear to them and has educational value.

2.6. <u>Detention on remand</u> should be only a last resort and restricted to exceptional cases, particularly where detention is in an institution intended for adults. Yet in some places it constitutes a short term of imprisonment.

---

[1] DELMAS-MARTY, Mireille. Modèles et mouvement de politique criminelle, Paris, 1983, Ed. Economica, p.13.

2.7. Imprisonment is criticised by most specialists if it is of long duration and served in ordinary prisons in contact with adult criminals. Centres specially designed for young adults or sections in reformatories for minors are preferred.

What is the value of short periods of imprisonment? Their opponents contest that they are of value for young adults while their supporters preach the merits of a short, sharp shock.

A suspended prison sentence along with supportive treatment may provide a salutary threat and assist the young adult; but if the suspension is repealed it raises the same problems as detention.

2.8. Today, sentences and measures in open or semi-open institutions are preferred in order to keep the young adult in touch with life outside. They may take very varied forms. Furthermore, half-way houses are springing up everywhere, as are small scale community facilities serving as a sheet anchor in the difficult situations sometimes experienced by young adults, whether delinquent or not. These places are often set up in response to specific needs; the forms of help they offer attempt primarily to campaign against institutionalisation and generally form part of social strategies.

2.9. There is unanimous stress on the need for the sentence or measure involving young adults to be accompanied by an educational framework allowing them to catch up on studies, occupational training, constructive leisure activities, a sport, etc.

Everywhere, stress is placed on the need for qualified staff to be with the young adults; staff must show themselves freely available and truly lucid about the task entrusted to them. There is much criticism of poorly motivated and overworked social workers and of the lack of co-ordination between the social services, the police and the courts.

2.10. In many countries there is a will to replace imprisonment by more positive punishment such as fines, prohibition from driving a motor vehicle, probation, etc.

2.11. There is no doubt that crime policy towards young adult offenders is a priority target in contemporary trends towards decriminalisation and diversion towards social strategies with all the advantages and disadvantages of such action. Care must be taken to prevent alternative measures from becoming automatic because of the age of an offender; conversely, their individual nature must be respected so that the educational value is maintained.

2.12 Today the traditional models of retribution and resocialisation are being replaced by new models which give a different meaning to the idea of punishment. These alternatives aim at settling conflicts and re-establishing the peace disturbed by the offence by remedying the harm caused by the offender. This revolutionary approach is particularly interesting in regard to young adults because it arouses their sense of responsibility by demanding a personal effort from them towards the victim and the community damaged by their offence (active repentance).

Community service work and particularly mediation follow this line and are often considered as sanctions in their own right. Highly qualified social workers and mediators are needed to apply them, because the task is a sensitive one in the face of often sceptical public opinion.

Application of these alternative sanctions raises a great many questions, including the following:

Are these diversionary measures? Should they be handed down by a court or decided outside the court system and without formal procedures? Should they be applied only in the event of minor or relatively minor offences or also in the event of serious offences? Should they be used for a young adult who is a first offender or in the case of further offences? Should the offender ask for the punishment himself (or through his lawyer) and can community service or mediation be imposed on him?

2.13 Criminology is in a state of turmoil and crime policy with regard to young adult offenders raises crucial questions for those who must formulate it. The time is therefore ripe for joint research and evaluation studies by European countries. Only close co-operation among them will permit scientific examination of the scope of crime and social policies implemented for young offenders and the preventive measures appropriate to them.

CONCLUSION

Beyond the choices already mentioned: special status for young adult offenders oriented towards the law on minors or towards general criminal law or law specific to the age group, a rather provocative question may provide interesting food for thought.

Why should criminal law and serving of sentences not be focused on the young adult age group while older criminals, who are the exception, would be subject to special provisions and prisons?[2] On many important points, the rapporteurs have differing opinions which will undoubtedly lead to animated discussion at this colloquium.

It would be an illusion to imagine that by the end of it unified model legislation or law for all countries on the continent will emerge. We have not yet reached that point! It is more important therefore to formulate joint lines of approach to crime policy with regard to young adult offenders while respecting the historical context of every member of the Council of Europe.

---

[2] BAECHTOLD, Andréa, Council of Europe Seminar at Spiez (Switzerland), October 1988.

NATURE AND EVOLUTION OF THE CRIMINALITY OF YOUNG ADULTS

REPORT

by
Mrs Jünger-Tas
Research and Documentation Centre,
Ministry of Justice (Netherlands)

1. Introduction

The great concern with crime is largely a product of the enormous increase in crime since the second world war in almost all western countries. However, the increase in crime is essentially a juvenile phenomenon: although the overall crime levels have been rising among adults as well as juveniles, juvenile delinquency has increased far more than adult crime.

This is shown quite clearly in figure 1 which compares the number of crimes committed per 1000 of the same age group for juveniles and for adults in Sweden. From 1945 on, figures for juvenile crime have been sky-rocketing, while adult crime figures are increasing much more slowly (Sarnecki, 1989).

Figure 1: Number of persons per 1000 of the same age group charged for serious crimes (v. Hofer, 1985; SCB, 1988; Sarnecki, 1989 - Sweden)

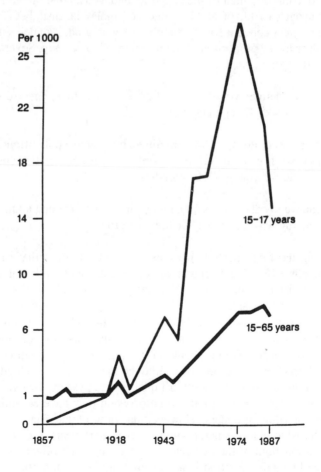

15

Considering the fact that similar changes took place in the other western European countries, it is of course no surprise that the major concern of authorities and governments was with juvenile delinquency, its nature, its prevention and its treatment. However, as Figure 1 also shows, at the end of the seventies - in some countries somewhat earlier, in others somewhat later - juvenile delinquency seemed to have stabilized and in some cases even to have decreased (Richardson, 1989; Tutt, 1990; Traulsen, 1988; Junger-Tas and Kruissink, 1989).

The consequence of this change in the crime picture is a slow shift in emphasis away from juveniles and towards the young adult population. It means the discovery of a new problem category and somewhat less focus on the old one. Thus the British Government's green paper 'Punishment, Custody and the Community' (July 1988) says on page 5 'The government is particularly concerned about young adult offenders, those aged between 17 and 20. In 1987, 99,700 young men and 12 300 young women were sentenced by the courts. Over 20 000 young men and 600 young women aged 17 to 20 were sentenced to custody. One in every 100 young men in this age group was given a custodial sentence. The Crown Court sends a higher proportion of young men aged 17 to 20 to custody than of men aged 21 and over. Young men in this age group account for about a fifth of all the sentenced males in custody'. The green paper clearly shows great concern for the number of young adult males sentenced by the courts as well as by the proportion of them sentenced to custody. Several questions will be treated in this paper, such as:

— How do we define 'young adult offenders' and, more precisely, what are the limits of this specific age category?

— In what respects does crime committed by young adult offenders differ from (adult) crime in general; in other words, is there a specific type of criminality characteristic for young adult offenders?

— What can we say about causal factors with respect to young adult crime; are these factors in any way particular for this age group?

Answering the first question we must take into account that in most western countries there is a clear legal separation between juveniles and adults, but the age of penal majority differs from country to country. For example in the United Kingdom penal majority is at 17 years, while in the Netherlands it is at 18 years. Germany makes an interesting distinction between children (under 14), adolescents (14-18) and young adults (18-21). In many countries there also exists some sort of 'intermediate' age category of 16-18 years. Young people in this age group are often considered on the fringe of adulthood and, in some cases, although they have not reached penal majority, they may be transferred to the adult criminal justice system. This may happen when they have committed a very serious crime or when they have committed offences in the company of adult offenders. However, in view of the fact that in most of the countries referred to in this paper, civil majority is at 18 years, I tend to consider 18/17 years as the lower limit of the age category of young adult offenders. With respect to the upper age limits the situation is just as unclear. Reviewing police statistics of five western European countries it appears that there is considerable variation: in Sweden and Norway the upper age limit of young adults appears to be 21, in England and Wales and (west) Germany it is 20, in Denmark it is 19 and in The Netherlands it varies between 20 and 23, depending on the analysis. The most realistic approach seems to be a non-dogmatic one, where the upper age limit of the young adult offender group is determined at somewhere between 21 to 23 years.

2. Some basic data on crime in Europe

Before presenting some basic data on crime in different European countries it should be emphasized that simple comparisons between countries cannot be made on the basis of police figures. Firstly countries differ in their definitions of what they consider criminal behaviour: for example some countries classify attempted killings in the category 'manslaughter', while others classify these in the category 'serious assaults'; some classify 'breaking in' as burglary, while others don't. It is clear that in this case any comparison between countries with respect to murder rates or burglary rates becomes very difficult. Secondly, countries differ in the way their police operate: in some of them the police have to report to the prosecutor every delinquent act they come across ('legality' principle), while in others they can use a certain discretionary power ('opportunity' principle). Thirdly, police registrations differ, both within countries and between countries. Fourthly, people - and countries - differ in their willingness to report offences of which they are victim to the police; some are more inclined to do so than others. Finally, police activity in order to detect crime may also differ within and between countries. The last factors have as a result that the extent of unreported as well as undetected crime - the so-called 'dark number' - is essentially unknown within any country, and, again, it may also vary in unknown ways between countries. Now this does not mean to say that police statistics are useless. When we are looking at long-term changes and developments they give a reasonably valid picture of such trends. Moreover, comparisons of police figures with other measures of crime, such as victimization studies and self-report studies, indicate that correlations between the three measures are generally high (Hindelang, 1981; Hindelang, Hirschi and Weiss, 1981). However, we should be careful when drawing general conclusions and limit ourselves to examine very global trends. A comparison of such global trends for the period between 1980 and 1989 has been made for seven European countries and Canada by three Dutch researchers (Essers, Kommer and Passchiers, 1991) on the basis of recorded police data. In order to avoid some of the difficulties just mentioned they distinguished only two broad categories of offences, property offences (including all forms of theft, fraud, burglary and fencing) and violent offences (including all forms of violence against the person, such as rape, assault - attempted and realized - and manslaughter).

Table 1: Recorded violent crime in eight countries per 100.000 population

	1980	1981	1982	1983	1984	1985	1986	1987	1988	1989
Netherlands	143	157	170	174	186	195	211	212	231	254
England/Wales	229	243	266	270	281	301	313	347	377	415
West Germany	372	389	384	386	372	387	389	388	392	-
Denmark	143	158	150	156	163	175	180	175	194	133
Sweden	360	353	405	417	441	457	465	490	528	563
Norway	112	124	124	142	141	152	151	169	197	-
Canada	618	635	654	602	642	675	725	769	799	846
France	135	149	166	175	186	188	168	162	-	-

Looking at Table 1, one can see a general increase in violent crime in all eight countries, although there are clear variations among them. The increase seems highest in England and Wales, the Netherlands, Norway and Sweden. It is lower in Canada and France. In West Germany the level of violent crime seems to have remained pretty much the same, while in Denmark - after a steady increase - the police figures show a sudden decline in 1989. With respect to the nature of violent crime, in the Netherlands two thirds of the offences are simple assaults and one third is theft with violence. Denmark has a similar distribution, but in the other countries - with the exception of France - 80 to 90% of violent offences are simple assaults and only 10% are thefts using violence. France is exceptional in that half of the committed offences are property offences implying the use of force. The following table gives an overview of the changes in property crime in the period 1980-1989.

Table 2: Recorded property crime in eight countries per 100.000 population

	1980	1981	1982	1983	1984	1985	1986	1987	1988	1989
Netherlands	3531	4124	4750	5193	5738	5773	5742	5773	5776	5684
England/Wales	4441	4892	5412	5314	5693	5798	6148	6161	5738	5900
W. Germany	4515	4850	5210	5272	4974	5108	5256	5346	5139	-
Denmark	7211	7144	7287	7242	7818	8251	8879	9084	9269	9255
Sweden	7517	7425	7777	7688	8128	8662	9307	9081	8992	9322
Norway	2545	2705	3069	3242	3049	3305	3295	3967	4325	-
Canada	5831	6155	6240	5984	5893	5849	5966	5983	5864	5760
France	3829	4232	5018	5205	5328	5182	4730	4504	-	-

A first interesting point to note is that in most of the countries studied property crime figures are some ten to twenty-five times higher than recorded violent crimes. Although we know that many violent crimes are not reported to the police because they are not considered serious enough by the victims, the conclusion seems justified that crime in western society is essentially property crime without any use of force. Looking at trends, it appears that in three out of seven countries, that is the Netherlands, England and Wales and West Germany, the number of recorded property offences seems to have stabilized since about 1985. This is not the case for Denmark, Sweden and Norway where there is still an upward trend. France is the only country showing a clear downward trend. Theft and embezzlement form the great bulk of property crime in all countries, although it varies from 78% of total crime in France to 97% in the Netherlands. Offences of deceit, fraud and fencing are on the whole more rare. Again, comparisons must be made with caution, because of differences in registration among countries: for example Denmark records 'joy-riding' as a property offence, while the Netherlands consider part of these offences as traffic offences. Concluding this very brief overview of the crime picture in some European countries, we might say the following. Firstly, crime in Europe is essentially property crime, mainly different forms of theft and embezzlement. Secondly the use of force is rare: only in a minority of cases is violence used when committing a property crime. Thirdly, not only is the level of violent crime considerably lower than the level of property crime, but the bulk of these crimes are simple assaults. Fourthly, where in most reviewed countries the level of property crime is stabilizing or even declining, violent crime seems to be on the increase - with the exception of West Germany and Denmark. Although we have seen that most violent offences are not of a very serious nature, this apparent increase may give cause to some concern.

3. Young adult offenders: official statistics and specialised studies

3.1 Some general information

There are different ways of measuring the involvement in crime by young adults. The first and obvious way is to examine police statistics. However, apart from the drawbacks attached to police data, unfortunately not all countries do present crime analyses according to age. In this section we will examine some available official data that will give us insight into the main crime trends in the western world. Let us first look at whether there are any discernable trends in the absolute number of young adults suspected for criminal offences in five countries. Again we should not compare countries, because some present data on persons found guilty, where others present data on persons suspected; moreover, the age categories differ.

Table 3: Absolute number of young adults recorded for criminal offences (x 1000)

	1985	1986	1987	1988	1989
England/Wales (18,19,20)	100,7	91,2	96,1	93,9	--
Sweden (18,19,20,21)	--	--	15,7	15,0	15,7
Denmark (18,19)	8,0	7,7	7,0	6,5	6,6
Norway (18,19,20,21)	4,0	--	3,6	4,1	4,9
West Germany (18,19,20)	151,9	152,3	147,0	41,4	--

A first fact to note is that in four of a total of five countries - with the exception of Norway - the number of young people suspected or found guilty of criminal offences has declined. This is probably related to demographic changes since the seventies: the declining birthrate in most western countries means that both the number and the proportion of young people in the population are declining. Fewer young people means also fewer offenders and this is shown in the statistics. A next question is how much of the total volume of crime has been committed by young adult offenders. This is shown in Table 4.

Table 4: Percentage of young adults of all recorded offenders

	1985	1986	1987	1988	1989
England & Wales (18,19,20)	17,2	17,6	18,0	17,9	-
Sweden (18,19,20,21)	-	-	17,1	16,6	16,2
Denmark (18,19)	13,4	12,6	11,5	10,6	10,3
Norway (18,19,20,21)	24,8	-	24,8	24,1	23,7
West Germany (18,19,20)	11,8	11,7	11,4	10,8	-

There are of course differences between countries related to the age categories covered and the level of judicial intervention reflected in the respective statistics. What is apparent, however, is a general decline in the involvement of young adults to the total production of crime (in England and Wales there seems to be relative stabilization). We may cautiously conclude that both phenomena are essentially related to changes in the age composition of the population, but other factors - which will be treated later in this paper - may also have had some effect.

3.2 Young adult crime in some specific countries

Sweden

According to police statistics the total number of suspected persons, aged 15 and over, has considerably decreased, from nearly 100 000 in 1982 and 1983 to about 90 000 in 1988. Police statistics, as well as victim surveys and self-report surveys have shown that the largest group of perpetrators are youth of 15 to 17 years of age; 19% of all suspected persons are aged 15 to 19 and 20% are aged 20 to 24 (National Council for Crime Prevention, Dolmen, 1988). This appears clearly in Table 5, which shows the total number of suspected persons as well as the number per 100 000 of the same age population, in 1988. It should be kept in mind that the Swedish population is about 8 million people.

Table 5: Total number of suspects by age group, and number per 100 000 of the same age group, 1988 (Sweden)

Age	Total suspected persons	Total suspected persons per 100 000 persons in age group
15-19	16 848	3 007
20-24	18 239	2 930
25-29	12 955	2 277
30-34	10 877	1 894
35-39	8 889	1 477
40-44	7 950	1 180
45-49	5 142	952
50-54	3 152	714
55-59	2 221	525
60-	4 151	214
Total	90 424	1 301

Highest criminal involvement occurs between the ages of 15 to 24 years, which is not very different from what appears to be the case in other European countries.

Young people aged 15 to 19 are suspected mainly of property offences, including auto theft and criminal damage. With respect to violent crimes and sexual crimes the age distribution is different and the average age is much higher (over 30 years).

With respect to violent crime the data show that violence is not widespread among the Swedish population. In a cohort of individuals up to age 26, only 4 out of every 100 were recorded for at least one violent offence. Many of those had a prior criminal history as well as a history of substance abuse. However, violence appears to be part of a much wider criminal history, dominated by various forms of property crime (Wikström, 1988). There is no evidence for the existence of a group of offenders committing exclusively violent offences. Perpetrators are usually younger men, although there is a relation between seriousness and age: those who commit serious violent offences or violence within the home tend to be older.

Sexual offences are generally not committed by young adults, the median age being 35 years. Persons suspected of rape had the lowest median age (32 years), while those suspected of indecent sexual assault against children had the highest (41 years)

(Martens, 1988). In 1988, 827 persons were suspected of sexual offences, of which 9, or 1% were women. In other words, sex crimes are extremely rare among women.

Robbery is not a typical adult crime. The median age for robbery is 25 years, but it is 29 for a bank robbery and 24 for robberies of a person (Lindström, 1988). Slightly less than 17% of suspects of robbery from a person were under 18 in 1988, and this proportion has remained the same for the last ten years. A majority of those suspected of robbery have a criminal history. Wikström found that 70% of suspects of robbery from a person had a prior criminal record. The large majority of robbery suspects are men. In 1988 only 7% of those suspected of robbery were women.

A typical young adult offence is burglary (Ahlberg, 1988). In 1988, 42% of known burglars were 20 years or younger. In 1980 this proportion was 54%, and it has been decreasing steadily since that date. This might be due to demographic changes as well as to a decrease in the clearance rate for burglaries. It should be emphasized that the risk of detection for burglary is rather low, so that the police statistics probably include only those offenders that are heavily involved in crime. Women represent 6% of the total number of known offenders, but they represent 10% of the number of suspects for residential burglaries.

Auto theft as well as thefts from motor vehicles are crimes committed very often by young men (Dolmen, 1988). Of those suspected of auto theft in 1988, 40% were 19 or younger and 21% were aged 15 to 17. A considerably higher proportion of young people commit these crimes than is the case for all other reported crimes. The proportion of female offenders is again very low. Of 4 600 offenders in 1988, only 5% were women.

Offences inflicting damage are mainly committed by juveniles. Wikström found in 1982 that 39% of those found guilty were aged 15 to 20, and that 7% of these were young women.

Drug offences are generally committed by persons aged 20 to 30 (only 9% of recorded offenders were aged 20 or younger). Female participation in this type of criminality is considerably higher than in the other types reviewed. The proportion of women suspected of drug offences in 1988 was 15%. However, drug offenses, by their nature, have a very large dark number (Knutsson, 1988), and it is difficult to have reliable estimates of the real extent of drug abuse.

If we consider the whole crime picture it may be concluded that young adult criminality differs in some respects from adult crime: it is less sophisticated and less violent and mainly concentrated on property offences. Typical young adult crimes are burglary, auto theft and theft from motor vehicles. Young women hardly participate in the crimes treated in this section, with the possible exception of drug abuse.

Apart from these data based on official criminal statistics, two specialized Swedish studies should be mentioned. The first is a longitudinal study in a large city (Stattin et al.,1989). The research followed a representative group of about 1 400 Swedish young people from age 10 to age 30 and used data collected from official sources. They found age for first adjudication was 16 years and 7 months. Considering all first convictions in the research group up to age 30, it appeared that 75% of them had already been convicted at age 20. Only one in four had their first conviction after the age of 20. Although the peak period of crime activity is 15-17 years, the broader peak period was 15-23. Because of the fact that most first offenders don't come back in court and that the most frequent offenders are not to be found in the youngest age groups, the average criminal activity per person was higher in the 18-29 age period than at earlier ages. The proportion of multiple offenders reached a peak at ages 18-20, where 12% of this age group were classified as frequent offenders.

The average number of offences committed up to age 30 was 6,9. However, 71% of those having a criminal record, were either one-time or sporadic offenders, which means that about one third of the offenders was responsible for most of the crime. In fact the top 10% most registered males in early adulthood were responsible for two thirds of all crimes registered during the twenty year period.

With respect to the nature of the offences committed the picture becomes familiar: the bulk of it is property crime starting before age 15; violent crime and alcohol-related offences start at later ages. Of all registered males between ages 15 and 30, 71,5% were convicted for a property crime and 24,5% for a violent crime.

The second study is based on crimes reported to the police and cleared. The study population consists of all those born in the Stockholm Metropolitan area in 1953 and still residing there in 1963. Police data were collected from 1966 (the thirteenth birthday of cohort subjects) to 1979 (their twenty-sixth birthday). Figure 2 gives an overview of age patterns and it confirms what has been found so far. The peak for crimes in the Stockholm cohort is 15-17 years with the highest incidence at 17. However, peak ages differ by crime type: for theft and vandalism it is 15 years, for fraud it is 21-24, for violence it is 19, and for other crimes 20.

Figure 2: Number of recorded crimes by age (Wikström, 1990; Sweden)

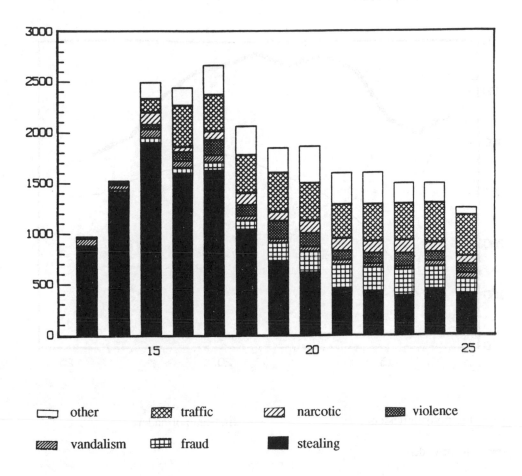

| other | traffic | narcotic | violence |
| vandalism | fraud | stealing | |

Wikström has also calculated the lambda's, that is the age specific crime-per-offender rates. For theft there is an increase in the crime-per-offender rate up to age 15, which then declines, while for fraud, traffic offences and violent crime, the crime per offender rate is just increasing over the ages.

The most interesting part of the study is the comparison between first offenders and recidivists. The comparison shows the increasing importance of recidivism with age. The number of first offenders continuously decreases with age, while the number of recidivists increases up to age 20, and then declines. However, the reduction in numbers of first offenders from age 20 to 25 is 64%, while it is only 23% for recidivist offenders. At age 17 more than half of first offenders are recidivists, at age 25 that proportion is 82%. Figure 3 clearly shows, as Wikström puts it: 'there is a decreasing input of new offenders'.

Figure 3: Number of first offenders and recidivist offenders by age (Wikström, 1990; Sweden)

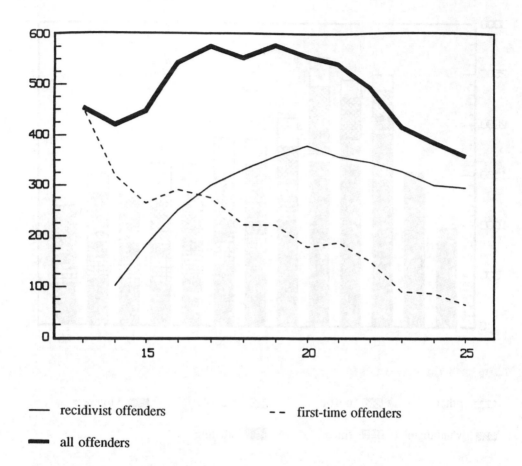

—— recidivist offenders   – – first-time offenders

▬▬ all offenders

Wikström also shows - in figure 4 - that regarding the number of crimes committed at each age, the recidivist offenders take on a growing importance. At age 15, 61% of all crimes committed at that age are committed by recidivists. But at age 25, 92% of the crimes in that age group are committed by recidivists. These results indicate that recidivists have a higher lambda, that is a higher crime-per-offender rate, than first offenders.

Figure 4:   Number of crimes committed by first offenders and recidivist offenders by age (Wikström, 1990; Sweden)

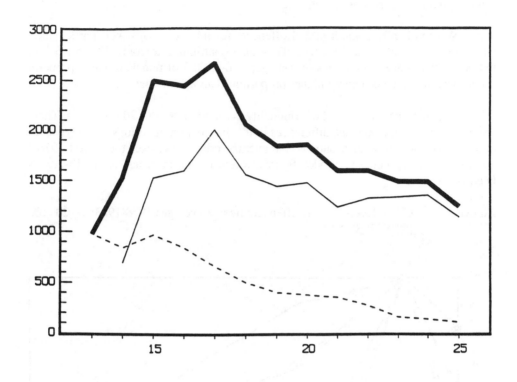

—— crimes by recidivist offenders   - - crimes by first-time offenders

▬ crimes by all offenders

The Netherlands

Between 1964 and 1983 the level of crime has increased for all age groups up to 50 years (CBS, 1987). The highest increase has occurred among those aged 12 to 25: crime involvement of these groups has steadily increased over the years. This is also the case for women: girls (12-17) delinquency has shown a threefold increase, while criminal involvement of young women (18-20) doubled. On the whole however, females account for about 20% of all recorded crimes. Public order crimes show a particularly high increase during this period: 8,5 times increase for those aged 12 to 17 and 4 times for the 18 to 20 age group, compared to a 2,5 times increase for all crimes. A similar remark can be made with respect to crimes inflicting damage: much of the increase here is due to juveniles and young adults up to about age 20.

As noted before, violent crime shows an increase and this is also true for property crime. The increase is however, the same in all age groups. Sexual offences show a clear decline, although this may be the result of a diminishing tendency to report certain categories of sex offences.

Women hardly commit sexual offences: for all age groups their participation was only 1% of all sexual offences. They also contributed for only 3% and 6% to public order offences and crimes of damage; in fact 80% of female crime is property crime, which is a considerably higher proportion than among men.

The highest relative level of criminality is found in the 18 - 20 age group. There are however, considerable age differences in the distribution of various crime types. In order to compare these distributions, the average crime level over the period 1976 - 1983 has been reproduced as index-figures, where the index of age group 18-20 has been fixed at 100.

Figure 5:   Crime levels of male offenders by age-averages 1976-1983; 18-20=100 (CBS, 1987-NL)

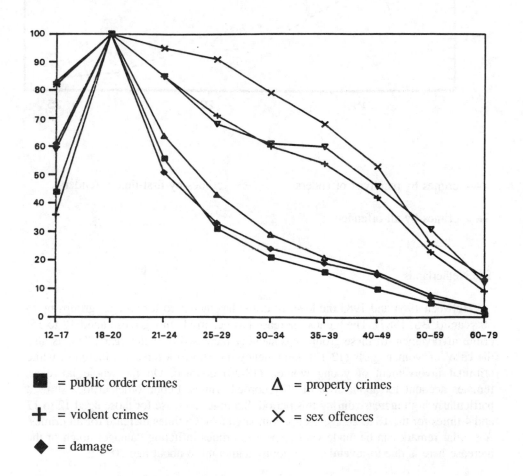

■ = public order crimes   Δ = property crimes

✚ = violent crimes   ✕ = sex offences

◆ = damage

Public order offences and crimes inflicting damage are strongly age-related. Involvement in these crimes is highest at age 18-20; at age 21-24 involvement has been reduced to only half of the reference group (18-20). A similar though less pronounced reduction can be seen with respect to property crime. Property crime levels are again highest for both age groups 12-17 and 18-20 and then decline quickly. Violent crimes - rare among juveniles - do persist for longer age periods and only slowly decline with advancing age. At age 40-49 violent crime is about half of the 18-20 years level. Sex offences are even less strongly related with age. Similar offending levels can be shown for age groups 12-17, 18-20, and 21-29, before a decline sets in. For women also the peak of criminal involvement is between 18 and 20 years. The crime level declines slowly: in age group 40-49 it is half of that of age group 18-20. It should be noted that this information is based on judicial statistics of 'persons found guilty'. No specifications are given about seriousness of crimes. This is of some importance because we know that most violent crimes of young people are non-serious simple assaults and sex offences are extremely rare anyhow. This will be better explained by looking at the crime distribution by age.

Figure 6:   Crime distribution of male offenders by age (CBS, 1987-NL)

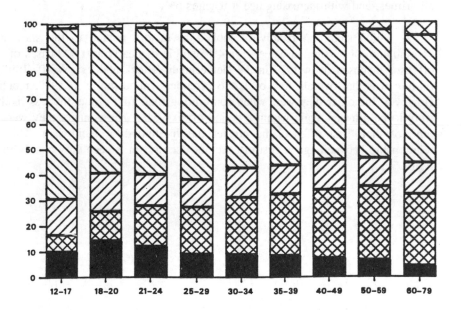

Figure 6 shows that public order crimes are of some importance in the 18-20 and 21-24 age groups, but the overall proportion of these crimes decreases with age. A similar conclusion can be made concerning offences inflicting damages and property crimes. With respect to property crimes it should be noted that they form the bulk of crime in every age group. However, there are some differences by age: in age group 12-17 property crimes constitute 70% of all crimes, in age groups 18-20, 21-24, and 25-29, the level is 60% and it declines to 50% at ages 60-79.

It is clear from figure 6 that violent crime constitutes a growing proportion of criminal involvement with increasing age. In age group 12-17 the level has remained at 6 to 7% of all juveniles found guilty of a criminal offence. In the other age groups the relative proportion increases with age, up to a level of about 30%.

Starting in 1970, sexual offences now form the smallest proportion of the total number of crimes. The absolute number of sex offences was three to five times higher in the sixties than in the seventies. Up to age 25 sex offences constitute only 2% of all crimes, and with increasing age it reaches 6%.

A Dutch study on recidivism looked at factors related to the start and the continuation of a criminal career in a 4% sample of nearly 150 000 cases of serious offenses disposed of in 1977 in the Netherlands (Block and v.d. Werff, 1990). One finding was that overall 40% of 1 456 offenders found guilty in 1977, recidivated. However, the older they were when committing their first crime, the less likely they were to be arrested again within a period of six years. The younger they were at the time of their first offence, the greater the likelihood of recidivism. This strong relationship between age at first offence and recidivism is seen very clearly in figure 7.

Figure 7: Percentage of re-arrests by age at first offence of males (Block and v.d.Werff, 1990; Netherlands)

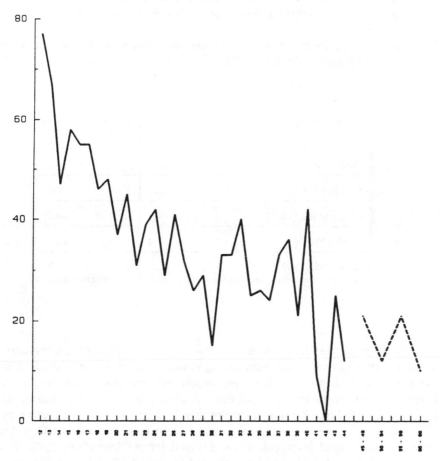

Percentage re-arrested within six years

Age at occurrence of sample 77 crime

The general trend is a decreasing curve from peak age 12 to age 60-80, although there are some variations from year to year. Of 12 year olds 77% were re-arrested within 6 years, of 21 year olds this was 45% and only 10% of men aged 60 to 80 were rearrested. Another finding is that age is less important as the number of prior arrests increases. For males who had had six or more prior arrests, the likelihood of recidivism was high regardless of age. This means that the most important variable is prior criminal history. For persons with six or more prior arrests, age is irrelevant.

Germany

The very elaborate and detailed German statistics (Bundeskriminalamt, 1989) essentially confirm what has been found for the other European countries. However, in view of their subdivision into *Kinder* (< 14), *Jugendliche* (14-18) and *Heranwachsende* (18-21), it is interesting to look at the distribution of crime between these age categories, compared to their proportion in the population.

Table 6:   Population age distribution and distribution of suspects of a criminal offense, 1988 (BKA, 1989)

	% population	% suspects
Children (< 14)	13,6	4,1
Juveniles (14-18)	4,8	9,1
Young adults (18-21)	4,8	10,3
Adults (21-25)	7,0	13,8
Older adults (>25)	69,8	62,7

It appears from these figures that the age groups of juveniles, adolescents and young adults are heavily over-represented among criminal suspects. They produce roughly twice as many suspects as their proportion in the population would warrant. Considering the share in the population of adolescents and young adults, we may conclude that the highest criminal involvement is to be found among persons aged 18 to 25. When we consider the changes that have occurred in the last five years, it appears that criminal involvement has declined for children (from 5,3% to 4,1%), juveniles (12,5% to 9,1%) and adolescents (11,9% to 10,3%). The consequence is that the proportional involvement of adults has increased (70,3% to 76,5%).

The finding that women constitute about a quarter of the total number of suspects is similar to what is found in other countries. This proportion remains relatively constant. Moreover, female criminality consists essentially of non-serious property crime and fraud, whereas men commit a greater variety of offences, among which are violent offences and public order crimes.

England

In many studies the data are drawn from publications of different national bureaus of statistics. There are, however, different types of studies focusing on the relation of age and crime. Most of these are cohort studies, which means that the researchers examine the criminality of specific groups of people born in the same year, over long periods of time. While doing this they generally make use of official statistics, but in some cases also of self-report data.

Thus an English study examined three cohorts, consisting of everyone born during one week in March, June, September and December in 1953, 1958 and 1963 (Shaw and Lobo, 1989). Considering the males born in 1953, fewer than 2% had their first conviction by age 12. Their first conviction rate then increased and was highest between ages 14 and 18. By the age of 21 almost a quarter had been convicted at least once. Thereafter the rate declined and at age 30 a third of the males had been convicted. The proportion of the males convicted in the 1958 cohort was 1% higher at age 20 and 2% higher at age 25. The proportion of males convicted in the 1963 cohort was higher still: at age 20 it was 1% higher than the 1958 cohort and consequently, 2% higher than the 1953 cohort. This would indicate a growing involvement of young men in crime or changing police practice over the years. However, in all three cohorts two-fifths of the men convicted before the age of 31 had been convicted only once.

The most common type of crime that led to a conviction was some type of theft; the second most common was burglary, followed by theft of a motor vehicle and criminal damage. Many studies found that the younger a male offender is at his first conviction, the more likely he is to be reconvicted (Farrington, 1989; Junger-Tas, 1988). Of those males first convicted between the ages of 8 and 14, two-thirds had further convictions within ten years and a quarter were convicted more than five times during that period.

Another English study examines the finding that the peak age of known offending, which was 13 before the second world war, has gradually been raised (Barclay, 1990). Although between 1976 and 1985 it remained at 14, it rose to 15 in 1985 and 1987, and reached 18 in 1988. Having no information on the background of this change, all chief constables were asked for comments. The answers to this request are interesting in that they shed light on some of the changes that have operated in most European countries. The chief constables indicate several reasons for the changing peak age:

— deterrence of shoplifters, based on the co-operation between the police and the stores;
— social crime prevention efforts;
— juvenile diversionary schemes;

We might add to this list the enormous increase in police cautioning (a formal warning, followed by a dismissal by the police), as well as the demographic factor (lower proportion of youth in the population). Farrington (1988) has based his Cambridge study in Delinquent Development on 411 males both on official and self-report data. On the basis of both data sources he found that burglary, shoplifting, theft report data. On the basis of both data sources he found that burglary, shoplifting, theft of and from motor vehicles, declined in prevalence from the teenage years into the 20-30 age group. This was not the case for theft from work, drug use and fraud. Farrington indicates that the relationship between self-report data and official convictions were strong for burglary, theft from and of motor vehicles, shoplifting, theft from machines, assault and drug use. Cumulated data over the period between ages 10 and 32 indicated that the probability for conviction was quite high for burglary and auto theft - over 50% - but lower for theft from vehicles -25%. The probability of conviction increased with age.

The United States

Because of the fact that the United States shares with Europe a similar cultural background, it seemed useful for comparative purposes, to summarize some essential data on criminal involvement of young adults in that country. For example in the U.S, as in Europe, young people make up the largest proportion of offenders entering the criminal justice system (U.S Department of Justice, 1988).

In 1985, two-thirds of all arrests and three-quarters of all Uniform Crime Report index arrests (for serious crime) were of persons under age 30.

Arrests of young people under age 21 made up half of all UCR Index property crime and almost a third of all violent crime arrests. Although the greater likelihood of arrests for young people may come partly from their lack in experience in crime and from the fact that they commit crimes that are more easy to detect - for example, purse snatching instead of fraud - arrest data seem to show that criminal behaviour declines with age. Figure 8 shows the general decline in arrests for serious crime with advancing age.

Figure 8:   Age and serious crime arrest rates (U.S)

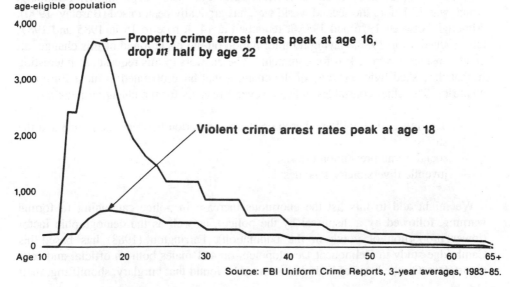

Arrest rate per 100,000
age-eligible population

Source: FBI Uniform Crime Reports, 3-year averages, 1983-85.

34

It is quite interesting to note that the relationship between age and criminal involvement is almost invariant according to time and place. Hirschi and Gottfredson showed that the age/crime distribution in England in 1842 is practically similar to that in 1965 (Hirschi and Gottfredson, 1983). Moreover, when comparing different countries, the authors found hardly any difference in that age/crime distribution. In fact the authors state that the relationship between age and crime is independent of variables such as time, place, sex and ethnic background.

The following figure gives an overview of the changes in arrest rates between 1961 and 1985 for different age groups.

Figure 9:   Trends in arrest rates by age group (U.S)

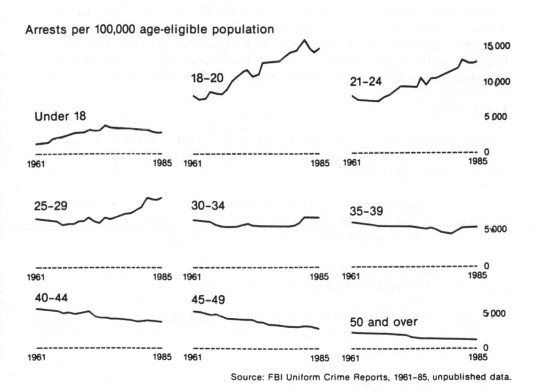

Source: FBI Uniform Crime Reports, 1961–85, unpublished data.

It is clear from figure 3 that, just like in Sweden, the most dramatic increase in arrest rates has been for the 18 to 20 age group, that is young adult offenders. There is a smaller increase in arrest rates for the 21-24 age group and even smaller for the 25-29 age group. Moreover, persons 50 or older had the lowest arrest rate, while young adults aged 18 to 20 had the highest rate, followed by the 21-24 age group.

Turning now to the relationship between age and the nature of crime, historical studies show that as adolescents grow into adulthood, they move more easily from property crime to violent crime (Cline,1980). Also the value of stolen property increases with age. But if we consider arrest rates up to an average age of 25 it appears that, with the exception of arson, all offences charged are property crimes. Although robbery might be accompanied by violence, it seems fair to conclude that in the US also, young adults commit more often property crimes than violent crimes.

Osgood and his colleagues (1989) used official statistics and self-report data in a large scale follow-up study among young people. They used four waves of data covering illegal behaviour between the ages of 17 to 23. Overall, roughly three times as many offences were reported by 17-year olds as by 23-year olds. 74,3% of males reported at least one offense at age 17, but only 29,7% did so at age 23. Although the peak age for overall arrest was 16 to 17, it was 21 for assault. Looking at time trends over the period from 1975 to 1985, there is a notable increase in assaults and a decrease in theft rates, especially in shoplifting. With respect to other offences, such as robbery, joy-riding, arson and vandalism, no clear changes could be observed. Osgood et al. concludes that arrest statistics and self-report measures are consistent in indicating substantial declines from 17 to 23 for practically all offences except assaults.

Conclusions

What may we conclude? The most important conclusion is that official data and self-report surveys produce on the whole a similar picture of young adult crime, which may be summarized as follows:

1. in most western countries the number of young adults suspected or found guilty of criminal offences has declined. As a consequence the proportional participation of young adults in the total production of crime has diminished;

2. young adults can be defined as the age group of roughly 16/18 to 23 years; all studies show that this is the peak period of criminal activity;

3. main criminal activities during that period include different forms of theft, burglary, auto theft, theft from vehicles, criminal damage; the prevalence of these crimes decreases between the ages of 20 to 30;

4. the prevalence of crimes such as theft from work, drug use and fraud does not decline after age 20;

5. violent crimes and sex offences are rather adult crimes: their prevalence increases with age and the peak period is much later. The crime-per-offender rate (lambda) for fraud, violent crimes and traffic offences also increases with age;

6. the younger a boy is when the first conviction takes place, the more reconvictions will follow: of those who are convicted before the onset of young adulthood, two-thirds will be reconvicted within ten years;

7. with increasing age, a growing number of crimes of the total number of recorded crimes are committed by recidivists;

8. the participation of women in recorded crime is considerably lower than that of men; their share ranges from about 17% (U.S) to about 25% (Germany and Netherlands) of the total crime production. Although criminal activity among young women and girls has clearly increased since the seventies, their offending behavior is still at a very low level. Women criminality is mainly restricted to property crime. Men are more likely than women to be arrested for the more serious crimes (robbery, burglary, rape);

9. the lower participation in crime of women has been a constant phenomenon. Although criminologists do not agree on its causes, there is some consensus about the importance of the differential socialization of boys and girls, implying more stricter social controls on girls than on boys. The reduction of these differences in recent times as well as a greater participation of women in education, the work force, leisure and social life in general, may be causally related to the relative increase in female criminality since the seventies.

4. Special crime categories

As we have seen, criminal activities of young adults are on the whole rather distinct from general adult crime. Some crime types appear to be typical for juveniles and young adults, such as football hooliganism, drug abuse and drunken driving. In the following section I will pay attention to these behaviour.

4.1 Football hooliganism

Violence related to sports events is not a new phenomenon. In the nineteenth century contests between young men from different villages usually led to fights and disorders. Horse races and football games were sports that attracted great numbers of spectators. Sports historians note that around 1870 football games usually were accompanied by riots, violence, fights and vandalism (Vamplew, 1983).

At the end of the nineteenth century the situation changes. In relation to higher incomes and more leisure for the labour population, commercial interests enter in sports. This leads to better regulation of sports events, because sport sponsors did not want to risk their financial investments by ramping vandalism. As a consequence sport grounds were fenced and partitioned so that spectators could be better controlled. Entrance fees were introduced and strict control was exerted on gambling, betting and alcohol use. Drunken spectators were not admitted. Special personnel as well as police force were hired to enforce these rules. However, in the 1960's and 1970's, commercial pressure leads again to more sports violence: the stakes in winning the game are so high that violence of players - especially in sports such as rugby and football - greatly increases. Spectator violence also increases, but as will be shown, is restricted to special categories of supporters (Dunning, 1983).

Causes of football hooliganism

Football in its organized form was born in England. It dates officially from the foundation of the Football Association in 1863. At first the game was socially restricted to the upper and middle classes and it was played in the English public schools by 'gentlemen' to be. But in 1850 the professional player was introduced, the popularity of the game increased, and at the end of the 19th century it had spread down to lower classes and became essentially a lower class game. Up to the 1960's however, spectators used to come from the 'respectable' working class, including mainly skilled manual workers. This changed in the sixties when football games started to attract also young people from the lower working class characterized by poverty and unskilled labour. Football hooliganism did spread to other European countries although not in all of them to the same extent. At this moment most of it occurs in England, Germany and the Netherlands. According to Dunning et al. (1986) lower working class communities generate values and norms that lead to or are tolerant of high levels of aggression. For example, boys from these communities are relatively free from adult controls and spend much of their leisure time in the streets with their peers. From an early age on they are socialized in the streets where patterns of aggression and a hierarchy based on age and physical strength develop. Parents are generally fairly tolerant of their childrens' misbehavior and when they intervene, it is often by physical punishment. So these children grow accustomed to - and are tolerant of - rather high levels of aggressive and even violent behaviour. Characteristic for these social groups is also sex segregation and a definite male dominance including high levels of violence towards women. In fact the males have a typical macho mentality, based on a strong group solidarity. They tend to enjoy fighting, it gives them status among their peers and some meaning to their lives.

Marsh (1987) considers football hooliganism as a ritual and non-serious form of aggression. Although outsiders might think that the singing, chanting and fighting has nothing to do with the game, Marsh sees these activities as meaningful and an integral part of the enjoyment of the game. According to Marsh the threats, counter threats and aggression are not very serious and have a social function. He makes a distinction between this type of aggression and violence that is not ritualized. In fact both these conceptions can be criticized: the existence of a clear lower working class subculture, condoning violence as a way of life and encouraging violent destructive behaviour in and outside sports grounds is questionable. There is no social group that supports and encourages violence, because it undermines social group life and social cohesion (Kornhauser,1978). The construction of Marsh might have had some appeal at the time that football hooliganism was restricted to shouting, threatening and other forms of non-serious behaviour, but unfortunately it does not explain adequately the actual forms of serious violent and destructive behaviour related to football matches. Without denying that elements such as obvious physical strength, the need for strong sensations, group pressures and status conferred by peers, are powerful incitements of violence, other considerations must be taken into account. Thus a Belgian study of Dunand (1987) emphasizes both the importance of the situation and socio-psychological variables in creating actual violence. The author indicates the conditions surrounding the Heysel drama in 1985: the anonymity of perpetrators in the mass of spectators, and their ensuing lack of feelings of responsibility; the outbreak of collective panic, feelings of powerlessness and intense emotions of anxiety among spectators, which leads to highly individual efforts to escape, without regard to others. She notes, based on empirical evidence, that the viewing of violence by players on the grounds is a stimulating factor in hooliganism, because it raises the hostility level. Following the Heysel drama a research group of Leuven University conducted an empirical study on football hooliganism in Belgium (Van Limbergen et al., 1987). They found that hooligans cling together in non-structured, loosely knit 'near-groups' in their respective 'sides'. Although there is no formal leadership, some of the boys are rather informal leaders. Most of the group members are genuine football fans.

Most researchers have paid attention to often cited 'causal' factors such as alcohol use and the role of the media. There is general agreement that both can be seen as precipitating factors but not as causes. It is true, of course, that alcohol has a disinhibiting effect. There is a strong relation between the abuse of alcohol and violent crime in general, but alcohol abuse cannot be considered as an independent cause of football hooliganism. As far as the media are concerned, there are quite a number of statements of hooligans indicating how much they value, enjoy and strive for publicity. Sensational coverage by the media means attention and recognition, producing high status among peers and there is no doubt that this kind of publicity has played a role in the spread of hooliganism in other countries. But again, although publicity gives hooligans a highly visible platform and consequently may stimulate hooliganism, publicity in itself does not cause football hooliganism.

There is one factor rarely mentioned by authors on this subject and that is the poor spectator facilities of so many stadiums (Williams at al., 1988). Not all dramas on the football grounds are the fault of hooligans! It is a sad fact that the Bradford City fire and the Heysel tragedy, that took place in 1985 and cost 95 lives, are for a large part caused by the appalling state and the poor facilities of the stadiums.

Who are the football hooligans?

English research in this field is mostly based on (participant) observation studies of a qualitative nature. To academics such as Williams, Dunning and Murphy, directing a research centre for football research at Leicester University, football hooligans are part of a larger 'skinhead' phenomenon. The aggressive skinhead style emerged in response to transformations of lower working class communities. Although not clear in the texts, the assumption seems to be that social and economic change produced in these communities high levels of unemployment and poverty, the consequence of which has been a cultural crisis and a falling back on traditional values of masculinity and gender, aggression and violence. One could say that, culturally speaking, these population sectors lagged behind other segments of the population (Williams et al., 1986). Whatever the merits of this explanation may be, it is difficult to test it by empirical research. In fact I tend to consider their theoretical contribution as a sort of background painting of historical and social change, affecting other behaviours as well. However, fortunately there are a number of researchers who have examined more closely the 'real' football hooligans, that is those who commit various violent offences.

These researchers (Zimmerman, 1987; Van Limbergen et al., 1987; Linckens and Berghuis, 1988; van der Brug, 1988) did establish the following facts. Firstly, as might be expected, football violence is essentially a men's affair, girls hardly participate. Secondly, average ages are 16 to 20 years, which covers the 'young adult' age category. Thirdly, football offenders are part of the traditional inner city street gangs. They sympathize with extremist right wing ideas, although this is partly simple provocation: interviews with hooligans indicate that they hardly know what right-wing extremism is about. They do, however, show considerable hostility towards foreigners, especially ethnic minorities.

Fourthly, many factors that have been operative in juvenile delinquency, are also valid in the case of football hooliganism, that is in those cases where violent offences are committed. For example, van der Brug tested the explanative power of school problems with an advanced statistical model (LISREL). The model explained 63,5% of the total variance of football vandalism. The Leuven research group found among football hooligans a lack of school motivation and of discipline, much truancy and low school performance. Zimmerman conducted research in Germany. He found that only a minority of hooligans had not completed their school education, but those who had not done so were more often involved in football violence than the others. Football offenders live in unstable or incomplete families, presenting many problems. Their parents are unable to supervise their sons in an adequate fashion. Many of them have unstable employment histories or are unemployed. They spend their leisure time mainly in the streets, in disco's and bars. Compared to ordinary football supporters, football hooligans have a lower participation in real sports activities.

But the most important finding is undoubtedly that football violence is not an isolated phenomenon. Football hooligans tend to show similar violent behaviour in other circumstances. Moreover, they tend to commit other offences as well. Three-quarters of the Belgian research group of hooligans had a criminal record at the level of the prosecutor. A Dutch study (Linckens and Berghuis, 1988) was conducted on 1000 persons suspected in 1987 of football-related violence. Half of them, that is 500 cases, were referred to the prosecutor. Of these 40% were minors and 60% were aged over 18. Half of this group had already a criminal record, mainly for property offences unrelated to football violence.

The inescapable conclusion must be that the hard core of football hooligans are ordinary delinquents. Football violence is just an expression of more generalized offending behaviour.

What can be done?

Various measures of a different nature have been taken, while others are still in an experimental phase.

Technical measures are among the first introduced. These include steel perimeter fencing, replacing standing-room by seated accommodation, the segregation of rival fans, the introduction of a system of football passes or identity/membership cards in order to control access. A number of control measures have also been introduced. Some are still in operation, others have been abandoned because they were too heavy a financial burden or failed to have any success. They include (massive) police escorts of fans to and from matches, the use of special railway disembarkation points in conjunction with police escort, legal restrictions on the carriage and sale of alcohol, the creation of a special club police force, searching fans for the presence of weapons and alcohol, a centralized and computerized information system on football offenders, exclusion of particularly troublesome fans from the games (in most cases the boys are required to report to the local police). In some cases, particularly in England, the judiciary have had rather extreme reactions, imposing heavy prison sentences on football hooligans.

Finally experiments have been set up with a social-pedagogical approach, or as others call it a community approach. Generally the approach is based on a social welfare ideology. The main idea is that the bond between the club and its fans should be strengthened, that problematic fans should be assisted in improving their living conditions and that the community should offer supporters a varied package of leisure occupations. Countries differ somewhat in the application of these ideas. For example, in the Netherlands eight communities, housing the most problematic clubs, have received state subsidies to set up social prevention programmes. In some of the cities the emphasis is on building a supporter's home, on stimulating a supporter's organization and on making a special leisure offer, such as outward bound activities. The best prognosis probably lies in a combination of repressive and preventive activities, where a youth- and welfare approach is combined with police and club control and offenders are subjected to diversionary schemes or alternative sanctions. This combination has been tried out in the cities of Utrecht (Netherlands) and Bremen (Germany). In Frankfort (Germany) a special football-loving team of police officers not only control fans at the games but they have permanent contacts with the young persons and help them in facing their personal problems. In England in 1978 the Sports Council supplied considerable funds to support sport schemes aimed at improving the relations between football clubs and their fans, and stimulating clubs to provide more sports facilities to the local community. For example the Manchester scheme provides a wide range of sporting and cultural activities, including a high commitment of the local football club. Unfortunately most clubs have only minimal involvement in such schemes (Williams et al., 1988).

Some clubs introduced seasons tickets and special membership sections; one of the largest clubs (Luton Town) introduced a comprehensive computerized membership card system, while at the same time no supporters outside the club's direct catchment area were admitted as members. This approach has been successful due to the collaboration of community organizations and local administration.

Finally it is appropriate to mention a Council of Europe convention on spectator violence at sports events, particularly at football matches. In June 1984 the sports ministers adopted such a convention, and in August the first six countries signed the convention. The convention mentions a number of measures that countries should take to curb spectator violence. For example, there should be sufficient police to guarantee peace and order; offenders should be appropriately punished; the clubs must make sure that hooligans should not be admitted to the matches; moreover, care should be taken that the conception and the structure of the stadiums should guarantee the safety of spectators; rival supporters groups should be separated; ticket sales should be controlled; supporters are not to be allowed to introduce alcohol in the stadium, nor objects that could be used for acts of violence. Three different procedures for the prosecution of football hooligans were mentioned: a) transfer of the prosecution for offences committed abroad to the country of residence; b) if necessary countries can ask the extradition of an offender; c) transfer of a sentenced offender to his own country to serve his term. However, the convention has essentially a preventive approach. Much attention is given to situational prevention, but also to social prevention requiring that members take adequate social and educative measures to develop in young people the sports ideal and the notion of fair-play (Sims and Tsitsoura, 1987).

4.2 Drug abuse

The situation in Europe

The study of drug abuse is complicated by the fact that use of illegal drugs belongs to the so-called victimless crimes, that is crimes that are not reported to the police by the victim, who is also the perpetrator. As a consequence police statistics about drug abusers are unreliable. The same is true for police seizures of drugs: does the quantity seized indicate an increase of drug use or merely a change in police priorities? Other measures are the demands for treatment to medical and social agencies, hospital admissions for drug-related illnesses, and drug-related deaths. All are estimates and we have no comparable and valid estimates of drugabuse in any of our countries. What we know is that massive drug taking - first cannabis products and later opiates, cocaine and amphetamines - slowly spread from the United States to Europe in the seventies. Cannabis and LSD were the first drugs used by middle class youth in Denmark, France, Germany, Netherlands, England and Northern Ireland, while amphetamines were preferred by working class youth in Sweden, England and Germany (Hartnoll, 1986). The heroin subculture emerged mainly in the large cities of western Europe such as Amsterdam, Copenhagen, London and Paris. According to Hartnoll the main general trends since the mid-seventies are the great increase in heroin use and the increase in drug abuse in countries such as Greece, Italy, Spain and Poland. Estimates are that in the Netherlands there are now between 15 000 and 20 000 addicts, a number that has remained much the same for the last ten years. Estimates of national drug officials amount to a total of 60 000 to 70 000 drug addicts in West Germany, and 60 000 to 80 000 addicts in England. Per 100 000 population the rate is 100 to 133 addicts in the Netherlands, 106 to 140 in England and 99 to 115 in Germany (Leuw, 1991). In all European countries the most frequently used drug is cannabis. Several countries (France, Germany, U.K) report the use of volatile solvents, but these drugs are mainly used by the younger age groups (12-16 years). Hard drug abuse is still very much dominated by opiates, although now cocaine is widely available. However, indications are that polydrug use is becoming more frequent. In the Dutch drug scene, and this could be the same in other European countries, part of the heroin addict population also uses cocaïne (Grapendaal, 1989). There exists some recreational use of cocaine among artists, musicians and party-goers, that does not have serious mental- or health-consequences and is relatively non-problematic.

There are indications that in cities with a longer drugs history, such as Amsterdam, Berlin, London, Paris and Stockholm, the average age of users is increasing, which could mean that the number of people starting a drug career is diminishing. On the other hand the use of drugs in smaller cities is still expanding (Hartnoll, 1986).

An interesting question is whether the use of cannabis is higher in the Netherlands, where there exists a pseudo-legalisation of the drug, than in other countries. In a recent study, comparing more than 20 Dutch prevalence studies with comparable studies in Norway, Sweden and the U.S, the authors concluded that 'A comparison with data from countries with a more restrictive policy reveals that the use of cannabis in the Netherlands is on the same level as in Sweden and Norway (around 10% to 15%), but far lower than in the U.S (exceeding 50%). However, the downward trend in these three countries since 1984 did not occur in the Netherlands (Driesen et al., 1989, p.11).

Some epidemiological data

There are several ways to study drug users: one is to conduct case studies, where special groups of users are approached; another is to conduct self-report studies among general populations, for example of young people; still another is to select the study population from persons seeking treatment. But as all methods have their drawbacks, the best policy is to have a combination of different research types. A Dutch prevalence study among a random sample (4 378) of the Amsterdam population of 12 years old and over (Sandwijk et al., 1988) inquired about the use of a number of drugs, including alcohol and tobacco, 'ever', 'last year', and 'last month', in order to get a picture of both long-term and recent use.

As expected the researchers found considerable difference between the use of tobacco and alcohol and the use of drugs such as cocaine, amphetamines, opiates and hallucinogenes. Tobacco and alcohol are first tried before the age of 16, while the first joint is smoked between 16 and 20 years. Heroin is taken for the first time between the ages of 18 to 21, and tranquilizers or sleeping pills are used by older persons (45 to 40 years). About a quarter (23,6%) has used cannabis, but the prevalence of the other drugs was low: cocaine use was reported by only 5,8%, the use of amphetamines by 4,6%, heroin use by 9,6%, and 3,8% had 'ever' used hallucinogenes. Another important finding was that 57% of cannabis and amphetamines users combined that use with alcohol, and 65% combined cocaïne with alcohol.

Cannabis was used first mainly by middle class youth with a higher education. This has been changing: as appears from 'last month' prevalence the drug is now used by lower class youth, the unemployed, military recruits, and students. Just as with delinquency, cannabis use is abandoned with increasing age. A similar trend emerges for cocaine: at first the use of cocaine was restricted to the bohemian, well educated 'jet set' between ages 25 to 40, but recently its use has spread among those with a weak social position (especially the unemployed and military recruits). In general it can be said that illegal drug use reaches a peak between 18 to 30 - for cannabis - and 35 - for cocaïne -and then declines sharply. Amphetamines and hallucinogenes are rarely used and mainly on an experimental basis. Heroin is generally used by marginal youths and abandoned after ages 35 to 40. Other - legal - opiates are more widespread and are used also in older age groups (>50). In this case women are greater users than men. Drug use is most frequent in the city centre and in the older parts of the city.

A number of studies use police statistics as the basis for their research. It is interesting to note that many of their findings confirm the self-report data. For example, a Swiss study on recorded infractions of the law on drugs (*Betäubungsmittelgesetz*) noted as the peak age of using drugs, 18 to 24 years. Women constituted only a small minority of drug offenders (Bodmer, 1989). Another Swiss researcher found that the use of cannabis, opiates and hallucinogenes is higher among young men than among women, but with respect to sedatives and sleeping pills women are greater users than men (Hornung, 1983). Considering drug seizures by the police, heroin is slowly replaced by cocaine, indicating a growing popularity of the latter drug. On the whole however, the drugs quantities seized per addict have substantially remained the same over the years. A German study of Hamburg police statistics found that mean offending ages are 18 to 25, and 78.3% of detected offenders are men (Schwanke, 1989). Sarnecki notes, in his study of Stockholm men, that of those with the worst criminal record (20 or more recorded offences before the age of 40), all had taken drugs (Sarnecki, 1987). The author also notes that the variables related to drug use are very similar to those related to delinquency. He found that men registered as intravenous drug abusers before age 40 tended to come from lower class families, where material and moral standards were low, where the emotional climate was hostile and discipline inconsistent and erratic. Moreover, the father was registered as an alcoholic. Other variables related to later drug abuse were school failure, the quality of leisure, the criminality of peers, and family dealings with social services. On the basis of this and other studies, the hypothesis that the causal factors related to drug abuse and delinquency are the same, does not seem too far-fetched.

Serious drug use and crime

In our own studies of juvenile delinquency we found a very strong relationship between criminal behaviour and the use of drugs and alcohol (Junger-Tas and Kruissink, 1989). Others have found the same for adult offenders. For example, Schwanke noted for Hamburg that, between 1977 and 1978, one in five addicts known to the police had committed a robbery and one in three a burglary (Schwanke, 1989).

Among the Stockholm men, 2% were recorded as drug abusers, but they accounted for 45% of the registered crimes; 64% had never taken drugs or only on rare occasions, and they accounted for only 13% of all registered crimes. Not all drug use is related to criminal behavior. Most cannabis users do not commit criminal acts. This has been shown both in Sweden and in the Netherlands.

The very strong relationship between criminal behaviour and drug abuse is no indication that it is the craving for drugs that leads to crime. On the contrary many drug abusers committed offences long before they took on drugs. Moreover, hard drug use can be financed by other ways, such as borrowing money, selling possessions, relying on a partner, social security benefits or prostitution. An Amsterdam study followed 150 serious drug users, of whom about two thirds were enrolled in a methadon programme (Grapendaal, 1989). The users were interviewed eight times during one year and their way of life was closely examined by a small number of researchers who were well known to them. What are their weekly expenses and what are their sources of income?

Average expenses per week are f 900 (± $ 450): f 65, or 7%, is spent on rent, gas, water, electricity, telephone; f 235, that is 26%, is spent on food, clothes, transport; and f 600, or 66%, is spent on drugs. The following table shows where the money came from.

Table 7:   Distribution of income sources of 150 serious drugusers

Social Security benefits	28%
Crime	22%
Prostitution	22%
Drugs market	18%
Work	4%
Odd jobs (black circuit)	2%
Other	5%

If one adds small drug dealing to the crime category, one may conclude that 40% of the income is the result of criminal activities (prostitution is no crime in the Netherlands). However, one of the major findings of the study is that drug use is elastic: users vary their drugtaking depending on their income. The view that an invariable craving for drugs presses the user to go in the street and commit some crime in order to fulfill his need is incorrect. The study found a very flexible pattern, where the available money dictated drug use: when the user was short of money he just took methadon to suppress withdrawal symptoms, when money flowed again more of it was spend on drugs. According to a regression analysis the following variables are related to criminal behaviour: sex (men commit more crime than women), age (the younger, the more crime), cocaine use (the greater the use, the more crime) and heroin use (declining heroïn use is related to more crime, but this is because heroin is replaced by cocaine).

In an English study, 300 offenders of burglary, theft, theft of a motorcar and criminal damage were selected from the police records. One third of that sample were known drug users, mainly heroin users (Parker and Newcombe, 1987). However, considering the distribution of their offences in the police records, the number of known drug users among car theft offenders and criminal damage offenders is much lower than expected. The number of drug users among theft offenders is as high as expected and the number of users among burglars is over one and a half times as high as expected. These results show that heroin-using offenders concentrate heavily on acquisitive crime. Furthermore there is a difference in criminal career between user offenders and non-user offenders in that the latter group has committed far more non-property crimes. On the whole user offenders have committed considerably more property crimes than non-user offenders. Another result, consistent with findings in the U.S, Sweden and the Netherlands, is that drug users and criminals live in the same neighborhoods.

One-third of the user group had no juvenile criminal record and started offending at a later age. This suggests that we should have a more nuanced view of the relation between drug use and crime. The study shows that the majority of drug users were committing crimes before they started to use drugs, but that in a minority of cases drug use led to offending. The authors conclude that in most cases heroin use is an extension of a delinquent career, but under certain circumstances of unemployment and poverty, drug use may lead to criminal activities.

These results are largely confirmed by a British observation study of a group of young addicts in an inner city area (Burr, 1987). All of them had committed a fair number of offences when juveniles; most of them had a history of truancy and unemployment. Their initial drug use was just one of their delinquent activities. Here too most of the offences were burglaries. Once they became confirmed users, their convictions went up and they did not seem to be deterred by custodial sentences. An interesting finding, which was confirmed by Dutch research, is that those who stopped or cut down heroin use, turned to other drugs, such as cannabis or heavy alcohol drinking. The spread of heroin use is related to the easy availability of the drug and the presence of local fences. But users, as a number of studies have shown, support their habit by all sorts of means: theft, wages, unemployment benefits and their families.

In fact there is much research evidence that drug taking is an extension of a deviant life style. For example Bean et al.(1988), studying drug taking in Nottingham, concluded that drug use does not lead to crime, nor does crime lead to drug use, but both are related to an illicit supply system. This system not only involves illegal drug transactions but also crimes related to those transactions. Hammersley et al. (1989 and 1990) concluded from their studies in Scotland that criminal experience and polydrug use were better predictors of crime than opioid use, and that in turn crime was a better predictor of drug use than drug use was of crime. In both studies drug use was essentially explained by crime, drug history and friends' behaviour. At this point some reference to American studies seems relevant, because they have a longer experience with the drug problem. Elliott et al. (1985), conducting large cohort studies, note that the causes of both crime and drug abuse must be found in the person's life history and social surroundings, rather than the one simply causing the other. Heroin use should be seen as part of delinquent behaviour instead of as the root of all other crime. However, they also note (1989) that although delinquency generally precedes drug use, drug use - especially serious polydrug use - subsequently influences criminal behaviour.

Summary and conclusions

On the basis of the available research evidence we arrive at the following conclusions:

1. Many legal drugs, such as tobacco, alcohol, tranquilizers and sleeping pills, are part and parcel of our culture and are widely used and abused;

2. The spread of illegal drugs over Europe started in the late sixties with the introduction of cannabis;

3. The prevalence ('ever' used) of hard drug use in a random population sample is very low and limited to some specific population categories. In most western European countries the average user's age is increasing, indicating a declining recruitment;

4. Cannabis use is more widespread than hard drug use: the prevalence of this drug may reach about 25% in a random population sample; however, cannabis use is not related to criminal behaviour;

5. Contrary to popular beliefs, the demand for hard drugs is elastic: it does not dictate frenetic criminal activities, but addicts adapt their use according to their available income;

6. Although users have a variety of income sources, such as family, unemployment benefits, prostitution, work and small scale dealing, there is a strong relationship between hard drug use and crime; most of the criminal activities related to drug use are property crimes (especially burglary);

7. The available research evidence shows that crime is a better predictor of hard drug use than drug use is of crime: most hard drug users have a criminal history, only a minority of drug users start committing offences after initial drug use;

8. There are clear indications that the causes of drug abuse are the same as those of delinquency: they must be found in an individuals' life history, family conditions, school past, employment history, and behavior of peers; drug addicts live in the same residential areas as most criminals, that is in inner city areas and in deprived neighborhoods.

4.3 Alcohol and crime

Alcohol is a widely accepted drug in western society. In the Amsterdam sample (Sandwijk et al., 1988) alcohol was first tried before the age of 16 and 75% of the sample had 'ever' used alcohol, making it's use a culturally 'normal' phenomenon. The excessive use of alcohol, however, may lead to behavioural problems. Thus it has been found that in the case of serious violent offences, such as homicide, serious assault, child battering and wife battering, as in the case of serious traffic accidents, the perpetrator is very often under the influence of alcohol. For example, research among convicted criminals showed that in a high percentage of cases of rape or serious assault there had been heavy drinking at the time of the crime (Rada, 1975; Mayfield, 1976).

There are however, some inherent problems in most of the research finding a relation between alcohol and crime, not unlike the difficulties that are apparent in the research on the relation between drug abuse and crime. Most of the research examines criminal convictions or police data on different types of crime and then looks at the number of cases where alcohol abuse was established. Apart from the fact that it is not always clear what criteria are used by the police to establish alcohol abuse, alcohol use is so widespread in the general population that a control group would be needed to demonstrate that the research group deviates from the norm. Moreover, there are essentially two different questions that have to be answered if one wants to establish a relation between alcohol and crime. One is whether criminals show more alcohol abuse than non-criminals, the other is whether alcohol abuse leads to crime.

Alcohol and aggression

An experimental study of Taylor and Gammon (1980) among university students showed that small amounts of alcohol consumption had a relaxing effect on subjects and did not lead to aggressive behaviour. However, high alcohol consumption led to frequent aggressive reactions to provocative behaviour. Increasing provocations by the 'victims' in the experiment clearly had a triggering effect on aggression.

A study of Leonard et al. (1985) looked at the effects of alcohol on fights and physical marital conflict, that is aggressive behaviour that rarely is recorded by the police. Using criteria developed by the American Association of Psychiatry they found that fighting was significantly related to a 'pathological pattern of alcohol consumption', to 'social consequences of drinking' and to 'signs of dependence'. Some 30% of those with a pathological drinking pattern, versus 14% of those without such a pattern had been in a fight since the age of 18. With respect to physical marital conflict the respective proportions were 25% versus 13%. Others (Coleman and Strauss,1979) showed that frequency of alcohol intoxication is a predictor of husband and wife physical abuse. In a review of the literature, van der Stel (1989) notes that alcohol impedes conscious and responsible decision making, thus lowering moral thresholds. This is clearly expressed in fights and in family violence (Vogt,1985). Alcohol diminishes abstracting and conceptual capacities, while the perceptual field is narrowed and coping mechanisms become less effective. If the situational context is perceived as provoking, complex interactions of cognitive, physiological and bio-chemical variables influence the emotional state of the user and increase the risk of violent behaviour.

The young, alcohol and crime

The relationship between alcohol and crime has been demonstrated by many studies. It is impossible, within the framework of this paper, to treat this topic in a thorough manner. I will just illustrate three questions that are relevant in this respect: 1. Is there a relationship between alcohol and delinquency in a 'normal' population? 2. What about the relationship between alcohol use and drunken driving? and 3. Is youth alcohol use predictive of adult drinking patterns? To illustrate the first point I refer to a self-report survey among the Dutch youth population of 12 to 18 years old. Drinking patterns and delinquency in a random sample of 1 120 subjects were examined (Junger-Tas and Kruissink, 1987). A total of 58% said they drank alcohol; among them three groups could be distinguished: 22,5% drank from time to time, 31% drank during week-ends, and 45,5% drank every day. Drinking was related with age: 63% of 15 years old, but 81,5% of 16- and 86% of 17-year olds drank alcohol. About half of drinkers and non-drinkers admitted to have committed offences, so in this respect there is no difference. However, if we take into account the frequency of drinking behaviour, we find huge, significant differences.

Table 8:   Alcohol use and admitted delinquency - in %

Offences	drinks little or none N=45	drinks at week-ends N=200	drinks daily N=297
fare-dodging*	17,5	38,0	23,0
shoplifting*	9,5	25,0	9,5
vandalism*	5,5	18,5	12,0
graffiti	12,5	18,0	18,5
arson	13,0	9,0	7,5
bicycle theft*	1,5	9,5	4,5
violent offense	22,0	22,0	19,0
burglary*	0,5	5,5	2,0
fencing*	6,0	12,5	9,0

* = $p < 0.001$

Those who drink at week-ends commit far more - and more serious - delinquent acts than the other groups. The differences are considerable and statistically significant.

Moreover, we found a relationship between soft drug use and alcohol use: twice as many soft drug users than non-users are weekend-drinkers (38% versus 19%). In fact our research shows that truancy, soft drug use and much (week-end) alcohol use are all related to frequent delinquent behaviour. These young people appear to have developed a 'deviant' lifestyle of which alcohol, soft drugs and delinquency are part and parcel.

A distinct problem is drunken driving, a form of behaviour that produces relatively many victims in the young adult age group. A survey among about 2000 15-, 16- and 17- year old high-school students in Queensland, Australia showed that as many as 10% reported to have driven a motor vehicle when drunk (Sheenan and

Nucifora,1990). The more often students drink alcohol, the higher the risk that they drive while under the influence of alcohol. The authors also indicate the influence of the peer group: the more friends the student has who drive while drunk, the more likely it is that he himself drives while drunk. Another striking finding is that those who drive while drunk favour activities that are exciting and risky (for example, parachute jumping). The authors also found that drunk drivers had significantly higher levels of delinquency. Finally, looking at predictors of drunk driving, the best predictor is drinking frequency. Other factors distinguishing under age drunk drivers from those who are not drinking and driving, are: being male, driving frequency, delinquency and number of drunk driving friends.

A crucial question in this respect is whether drinking patterns of young people predict adult drinking, or in other words do experiences with drinking in early life determine later life drinking behaviour?

If this is the case then early intervention would prevent later adult drinking problems. In a review of the literature on youth drinking behaviour, Kandel distinguishes three groups of variables: socio-demographic variables (sex, age, ethnicity, SES...); psychological and personality variables, attitudes and values; interpersonal variables referring to family and peers (Kandel, 1980). Although these variables do explain youth drinking behaviour quite adequately, the question of whether adolescent drinking patterns persist through life can only be resolved by longitudinal research. Two researchers from Berkeley University (Temple and Middleton Fillmore, 1986) have followed a sample of high school male students in a medium-sized county from age 16 to age 31 by means of yearly questionnaires on drinking behaviour. At age 21 roughly half of the sample reported drinking regularly or occasionally 'to get high', while at age 31 the proportion is 43%. The most heavy and problematic drinking occurs at ages 18 to 24, which parallels the peak delinquency period.

Table 9 shows the changes in drinking behaviour over time.

Table 9: Relationship between drinking at age 18 (1967) and drinking at age 31 (1979)

1967 drinking status	N (%) in each 1979 drinking status			
	Abstainer	Seldom get high	Regularly get high	Total
Abstainer	12 (15)	41 (51)	27 (34)	80 (100)
Seldom get high	4 (4)	46 (47)	48 (48)	98 (100)
Regularly get high	4 (7)	23 (43)	27 (50)	54 (100)

Table 9 essentially shows the absence of continuity in drinking behaviour: roughly half of the groups changed their behaviour. Moreover, less than half of them drank regularly at age 31, regardless of their past drinking behaviour. One of the conclusions of the authors is that drinking and drinking problems among young men is of an experimental nature and therefore unstable and unpredictable. The strongest predictor of adolescent drinking was the association with negatively oriented peers, while high school performance, family social class and family support were more important in later years. In fact most of the young men drinking regularly at age 18 had 'matured out' by the age of 31.

The major conclusion that I would draw on the basis of the research literature is that alcohol abuse, drug abuse and delinquency are related, that the main predictors of each of them are similar and that in most cases these deviant and risky forms of behaviour are seriously reduced or abandoned by the age of 30. Research shows that those who persist in these forms of behaviour form a small, albeit seriously criminal, sub-group.

5. Conclusions and recommendations

-    young adult offenders (16/18 to 23) form a special category: their criminality differs from that of juveniles as well as from that of adults;

-    the number of young adults suspected or found guilty of criminal offences has declined. This is essentially due to changes in the population age composition;

-    young adult crime consists mainly of property crimes: thefts, including theft of and from automobiles and burglary. The prevalence decreases between the ages 20 to 30;

-    the prevalence of violent crimes and sex offences increases with age: these crimes are characteristic of adults and their peak period is at later ages. Lambda, or the crime-per-offender rate for fraud, violent crimes and traffic offences also increases with age;

-    age at first conviction predicts later criminal involvement: two thirds of those convicted before young adulthood will be reconvicted within ten years;

-    although female participation in crime is much lower than that of men, female criminality has increased in the last 10 to 15 years. The increase may be related to the increasing participation of women in social and economic life;

-    alcohol abuse, drug abuse and criminal behavior are strongly related and have similar predictors. They are expressions of a deviant life style and tend to decline together between age 20 and 30;

Finally, it seems to me this paper has three major policy implications:

Firstly, in view of the changes that have occurred in Europe and the necessity of an ever closer collaboration between the European member states, it is urgent that the scientific community develops common research instruments so that we will be able to compare among states not only crime levels and crime patterns, but also backgrounds and causal explanations and the effectivity of differential intervention strategies.

Secondly, in order to have an impact on young adult crime, we should plead for a heavy emphasis on prevention. The reason for this is that although indeed young adulthood is the peak period of criminal involvement, the activities are predominantly property crimes. This type of crime can be reduced by different prevention strategies.

Technical preventive devices have been successfully applied in housing estates (reducing vandalism and burglary), in football stadiums, in shops and in public buildings. Situational crime prevention, for example in the form of supervision in shopping centres and housing estates and more control in the public transport system, has also been introduced with positive results. Social crime prevention strategies have been tried in the school system and in deprived communities. As far as young adults are concerned we should think of vocational training and work projects. These might be imposed in the form of diversion, in order to avoid prosecution or even as an alternative sanction. This type of intervention would have to be tried out, especially with young members of ethnic minority groups, where lack of schooling and unemployment are considerable.

Thirdly, in view of the nature of young adult criminality in general, prison sentences do not seem the most adequate punishment. In most cases any alternative is a better option. In the Netherlands good results in terms of reconviction have been obtained with community service for young adult property offenders (Bol and Overwater, 1986). Experiments are being conducted in several European countries with different types of training programmes, ranging from information (drunken driving) and social skills training to professional training and work projects. The United States and the United Kingdom have introduced intensive probation supervision, which allows for a highly individualized programme in the community, including combinations of community service, counselling, treatment (in the case of drug abuse), training, payment of damages -all under very close supervision of a probation worker. Prison should be reserved for a small group of highly violent offenders. In all other cases sanctions in the community are preferable and should continue to be created.

BIBLIOGRAPHY

Ahlberg, J
"Burglary"
In: *Crime trends in Sweden*, ed. L. Dolmen
National Council for Crime Prevention, 1988

Barclay, G.C.
"The peak age of known offending by males"
Research Bulletin of Home Office, Research and Planning Unit, N0. 28, 1990

Bean, P.T. and Chr.K. Wilkinson
"Drug-taking, crime and the illicit supply system"
British Journal of Addiction, 83, 1988

Block, C.R. and C. v.d. Werff
"Initiation and continuation of a criminal career"
Den Haag, Ministerie van Justitie, WODC, N0 105, 1991

Bodmer, M.
"Drogen und Kriminalität"
Kriminologisches Bulletin, vol. 15, N0 2, 1989

Bol, M. en J. Overwater
"Recidive van dienstverleners"
Ministerie van Justitie, WODC, N0 73, 1986

Burr, A.
"Chasing the dragon: heroin misuse, delinquency and crime in the context of south London culture"
British Journal of Criminology, vol.27, N0 4, 1987

Cline, H.F.
"Criminal behaviour over the life span"
Constancy and Change in human development, O.G. Brim, J.Kagan eds.,
Cambridge, Mass; Harvard Univ. Press, 1980

Coleman, D.H. and M.A. Strauss
"Alcohol abuse and family violence"
Paper presented at the annual meeting of the American Sociological
Association, Boston 1979

Dolmen, L.
"Theft of and from motor vehicles"
Crime trends in Sweden, ed. by L. Dolmen
National Council for Criminal Prevention, 1988

Dunand, M.A.
"Violence et panique dans le stade de football de Bruxelles en 1985: approche psychosociale des événements"
Revue de Droit pénal et de Criminologie, vol. 69, NO 5, 1987 nr.5, 1987

Dunning, E.
"Social bonding and violence in sport: a theoretical-empirical analysis"
Sports violence, ed. by J.H. Goldstein
New York, Springer Verlag, 1983

Dunning, E., P. Murphy and J. Williams
"Spectator violence at football matches: towards a sociological explanation"
British Journal of Sociology, vol. 37, NO 2, 1986

Elliott, D.S., D. Huizinga and S.S. Ageton
Explaining delinquency and drug use
London, Sage, 1985

Elliott, D.S., D. Huizinga and S. Menard
Multiple problem Youth - delinquency, substance use and mental health problems
New York, Springer Verlag, 1989

Essers, J., M. Kommer en I. Passchier
"De ontwikkeling van de geregistreerde criminaliteit in acht landen"
SEC, jrg. 5, januari 1991

Farrington, D.P.
"Self-reported and official offending from Adolescence to adulthood"
Self-report Methodology in Criminological Research,
ed. by M.W. Klein, Boston, Kluwer-Nijhof, 1988

Farrington, D.P.
"The origins of crime; the Cambridge study of delinquent development"
London, Home Office Research and Planning Unit Bulletin, NO 27, 1989

Grapendaal, M.
"De tering naar de nering: middelengebruik en economie van opiaatverslaafden"
Justitiële Verkenningen, vol.15, NO 5, 1989

Hammersley, R. and V. Morrison
"Effects of polydrug use on the criminal activities of heroin users"
British Journal of Addiction, 82, NO 8, 1987

Hammersley, R.et.al.
"The relationship between crime and opioid use
British Journal of Addiction, 84, NO 9, 1989

Hammersley, R. et.al.
"The criminality of new drug users in Glasgow"
British Journal of Addiction, 85, NO 12, 1990

Hartnoll, R.L.
"Current situation relating to drug abuse assessment in European countries"
Bulletin on Narcotics, 28: 65-80, 1986

Hindelang, M.J.
"Variations in sex-race-age specific incidence rates of offending"
American Sociol. Review, vol. 46, 1981

Hindelang, M., Tr. Hirschi and J. Weis
Measuring delinquency
Beverley Hills, Sage, 1981

Hirschi, Tr. and M. Gottfredson
"Age and the explanation of crime"
American Journal of Sociology, vol. 89, NO 3, 1883

Hornung, R.
Drogen in Zürich
Bern, Verlag Hans Huber, 1983

Junger-Tas, J.
"Causal factors: social control theory"
Juvenile delinquency in the Netherlands
ed. by J.Junger-Tas and R. Block Berkeley, Amstelveen, Kugler Publications,
1988

Junger-Tas, J. en M. Kruissink
"De ontwikkeling van de jeugdcriminaliteit: 1980-1988"
Den Haag, Ministerie van Justitie, WODC, 1990

Kandel, D.
"Drug and drinking behaviour among youth"
Ann. Rev. Sociol. 6, 1980

Kornhauser, R.R.
Social sources of delinquency: an appraisal of analytic models
Chicago, University of Chicago Press, 1978

Leonard, K.E. et.al.
"Patterns of alcohol use and physically aggressive behaviour in men"
Journal of Studies on Alcohol, vol. 40, N0 4, 1985

Leuw, E.
"Drugs and drug policy in the Netherlands"
Paper presented at a seminar of the Rand Corporation
California, U.S.A., May 1991

Mimbergen, K. van, C. Colaers en L. Walgrave
"De maatschappelijke en socio-psychologische achtergronden van het voetbalvandalisme"
K.U. Leuven, faculteit der Rechtsgeleerdheid, 1987

Lindström, P.
"Robbery"
Crime trends in Sweden, ed. by L. Dolmen
National Council for Crime Prevention, 1988

Martens, P.
"Sexual Crimes"
Crime trends in Sweden, ed. by L. Dolmen
National Council for Crime Prevention, 1988

Marsh, P., E. Rosser and R. Harre
The rules of disorder - London, 1978

Mayfield, D.
"Alcoholism, alcohol, intoxication and assaultive behaviour"
Diseases of the nervous system, vol. 37, 1976

Osgood, D.W., P.M. O'Malley, J.G. Bachman and L.D. Johnston
"Time trends and age trends in arrested and self-reported illegal behaviour"
Criminology, vol. 27, N0 3, 1989

Parker, H. and R. NewCombe
"Heroin use and acquisitive crime in an English community"
British Journal of Sociology, vol. 38, N0 3, 1987

Rada, R.T.
"Alcoholism and forcible rape"
American Journal of Psychiatry, vol. 132, N0 4, April 1975

Richardson, N.
"Justice by geography - legislation, demography and decision-making"
Social Information system, Manchester, U.K., 1989

Sarnecki, J.
"The connection between drug abuse and crime"
Conference on the reduction of urban insecurity
Council of Europe, November 1987

Sarnecki, J.
"Juvenile delinquency in Sweden"
National Council for Crime Prevention, 1989

Sheehan, M. and J. Nucifora
"The young, delinquency, drink and driving
Alcohol and crime; conference proceedings
Australian Institute of Criminology, Canberra, 1989

Schwanke, J.
"Die Beschaffungskriminalität von rauschgiftabhängigen in Hamburg"
Kriminalistik, NO 3, 1989

Shaw, K. and D. Lobo
"Criminal careers of those born in 1953, 1958 and 1963"
London, Research Bulletin, Home Office Research and Planning Unit, NO 27,
1989

Sims, P.N. and A. Tsitsoura
"La Convention européenne sur la violence et les débordements des spectateurs
lors des manifestations sportives et notamment les matches de football"
Revue de Droit pénal et de Criminologie, vol. 69, NO 5, 1987

Stattin, H., D. Magnusson and H.Reichel
"Crime activity at different ages"
British Journal of Criminology, vol. 29, NO 4, Autumn 1989

Stel, J.C. van der
"Alcohol en Criminaliteit: aandacht voor agressie en geweld"
Justitiële Verkenningen, vol. 15, NO 5, 1989

Taylor, S.P. and C.B. Gammon
"Effects of type on dose of alcohol on human physical aggression"
Journal of Personality and Social Psychology, vol. 32, NO 1, 1980

Temple, M.T. and K. Middleton Fillmore
"The variability of drinking patterns and problems among young men,
age 16-31: a longitudinal study"
The International Journal of Addictions, 20, 1985-1986

Traulsen, M.
"Eine Theorie ging an der Wirklichkeit vorbei; der Geburtenrückgang und seine Auswirkungen auf die Kriminalitätsbelastung junger Menschen"
Kriminalistik, Juli 1988

Tutt, N.
"The future of the juvenile justice system"
The future of the juvenile justice system
ed. by J. Junger-Tas, L. Boendermaker and P. van der Laan, Leuven, 1990

U.S. Department of Justice
Report to the Nation on Crime and Justice
March 1988

Vamplew, W.
"Unsporting behaviour: "The control of football and horse-racing crowds in England, 1875-1914""
Sports violence, ed. by J.H. Goldstein
New York, Springer Verlag, 1983

Vogt, I.
Macht Alkohol gewalttätig? Über den Zusammenhang von Alkohol und Delinquenz Drogalkohol, N0 9, 1985

Williams, J., E. Dunning and P. Murphy
The rise of the English soccer hooligan
Youth and Society, vol. 17, N0 4, 1986

Wikström, P.O.H.
"Violent Crimes"
Crime trends in Sweden, ed. by L. Dolmen
National Council for Crime Prevention, 1988

Wikström, P.O.H.
"Age and Crime in a Stockholm Cohort"
Journal of Quant. Criminology, vol. 6 N0 6, N0 1, 1990

THE SOCIAL STATUS OF THE YOUNG ADULT
(PSYCHOLOGICAL AND SOCIAL CHARACTERISTICS,
SOCIAL IMAGE, SPECIFIC PROBLEMS OF YOUNG ADULT MIGRANTS)

REPORT

by
Mr G. MAUGER,
Researcher,
CNRS, (France)

I. ASPECTS OF THE SOCIAL STATUS OF YOUNG ADULTS

A.   Problems of definition

Age classifications, like any form of social categorisation, are the product of a process of delimitation, definition, identity construction and representation. Although they are closely interlinked, it is convenient to distinguish three types of definition: political definitions, scientific definitions, and ordinary cognitive definitions, for which there are three corresponding types of distinct but interdependent activity: the political task of constructing collective identities, the scientific task of defining categories, and the task of identification which everyone carries out in everyday life.[1] Distinct though these definitions and the images corresponding to them may be, they are obviously not independent: for example, attention should be drawn to the extent of the dependence of political definitions on ordinary perceptions and scientific perceptions, as well as the extent to which the same ordinary perceptions are themselves dependent on political definitions and scientific definitions and so on.

1.   The political definitions

Over the last three centuries, the political authorities, whatever their form, have classified individuals or citizens according to age, thereby establishing increasingly precise regulations based on age (on the model of the *Ancien Régime*).[2] Very early on, the military authorities defined categories of recruitment and mobilisation (ranging from the so-called "maritime enrolment" system to that of conscription). The political authorities contributed to this process by defining an electoral majority and age limits for the right to stand for the various electoral mandates. Increasingly detailed regulations laid down lower and upper age limits for access to the labour market. It is no doubt the schools, however, which have done the most to institutionalise the age factor, by setting an age for entry into the school system, matching age groups with classes, establishing a compulsory school leaving age, lower and, more especially, upper age limits for various entrance examinations, and so on. Lastly, the law lays down age qualifications for civil, civic and penal majority, which are nearly always different.

2.   The scientific definitions: biological, psychological, sociological

Age, as officially recorded, is a measurement of the time elapsed since birth. L. Thévenot writes that "this is the ideal statistical variable: (...) universal and timeless, quantitative, in short naturally mathematical, it is available as such for all comparisons and all calculations".[3] This registered age, the measurement of which coincides with that of time, makes it possible to place on the same scale the stages of the various aspects of ageing: biological, psychological and social. The study of the different aspects of ageing leads to a definition of relatively independent chronological sequences: the Freudian or Piagétian stages, biological cycles, stages in social life.[4] Can youth be defined in sociological terms as a "stage of life" (between childhood and adulthood) with specific psychological characteristics?

A life history may be described as a set of career patterns in various institutional settings which are themselves in a state of perpetual flux. Thus, any attempt to identify the cycles of a life history must take account of two distinct but relatively interdependent types of event: "individual events" which mark the different stages of a life history (but whose recurrent features reflect the history of social structures), and "historical events" which punctuate the development of social structures (and which leave their mark on individual career patterns).

Let us suppose that these life histories unfold in the context of immutable structures. It is then necessary to identify the significant individual events of the different stages of a career through life. But what stages and what events will be selected? It would of course be futile to venture to draw up an exhaustive catalogue of the sequences, institutional or otherwise, through which the range of life histories might pass, and even more futile to seek to survey all the "meaningful moments" of the different career patterns concerned. Study is usually confined to the family, educational and occupational circles, because they exert the most clear-cut, constant and widespread socialising influence. Individual educational careers reflect the identification of institutional periods within the different cycles. Occupational careers may be easily identified on the basis of the succession of jobs. While the path followed in the family of origin may be described as a process of gradual emancipation, it is more difficult to identify the stages in that process. Three aspects are usually singled out: the achievement of financial independence, finding one's own home and the descent of an estate. As regards the founding of a family by procreation, this is the result of one or more trial periods of variable duration (engagement and/or cohabitation), which may or may not culminate in marriage and/or the birth of the first child. How is it possible, in the context of this simplified description, to provide a definition sufficiently stable and coherent to enable comparisons to be made in time and social space, that is to say one which has synchronic relevance to the entire social space considered and diachronic relevance to two separate periods of time? In order to satisfy this logical constraint, it is necessary to forego the search for "borderline events" which, at the outset, would separate "youth" from "childhood" (such as school leaving or departure from the family of origin) and which, at a later stage, would mark the coming of adulthood (such as accession to working life or marriage).[5] It is thus necessary to look for stable processes rather than fixed points of reference. Accordingly, it may be considered that youth is the stage of life at which a dual transition occurs: from school to occupational activity and from the family of origin to the procreative family.

B.   Some aspects of contemporary trends in the condition of young adults

In seeking to review contemporary trends in the condition of young adults or, in other words, trends affecting the different forms of the dual transition from school to occupational activity and from the family of origin to the procreative family, it is first necessary to identify the principal changes, structural and/or cyclical, in the educational system, the labour market and family structures in Europe.

1.   Factors contributing to contemporary trends

The growing demand for a school education (which is also increasingly expressed by working class families) is responsible for the extension of compulsory schooling beyond the age of 16 almost everywhere in Europe, as well as the resulting surfeit of educational diplomas and the plunge in their value which particularly affects lower-level diplomas in the field of technical education. Moreover, since the second half of the 1970s, the economic crisis affecting all European countries (in varying degrees) has spawned both unemployment and insecurity of employment: unskilled or underskilled young people are the first victims of this phenomenon. The disappearance of entire sectors of industrial employment (mining, metalworking, textiles, etc.) leads to the disappearance of traditional manual trades, the devaluation of technical diplomas which provided access to such trades, the depreciation of physical strength (as an employment asset) and of the "masculine values" which go with it and which occupied a central position in the workshop culture (and, more generally speaking, in the definition of the traditional masculine identity in working class circles). This also explains the decline of the traditional workers' movement and of its values, and the concurrent rehabilitation of money and of financial success as a criterion of social success. Lastly, the dissemination of contraceptive techniques, the legalisation of abortion and the general liberalisation of the moral climate no doubt help to account for the growing demand for independence on the part of young adults and the increase in cohabitation in their ranks.

2.   Trends in the condition of the young adult

For young people of both sexes, the prolongation of compulsory schooling and the general extension of school life in the context of the long-term history of the educational system have deferred the stage at which individuals join the workforce. Moreover, the extension of unemployment and the increasing incidence of insecure jobs, together with the resulting growth of measures to promote the social and occupational integration of young people since the second half of the 1970s, have diversified the forms of transition from childhood to adulthood. For a not inconsiderable proportion of young people who leave school at the age of about 18 or 19 with devalued technical diplomas, vocational integration always takes place shortly after they leave school, and the period of young adulthood corresponds more or less to the traditional pattern. However, for those young people who leave school with no vocational training at the end of their compulsory schooling and for some of those holding "devalued" diplomas, a new form of transition from school to occupational activity is making its appearance. Whereas, traditionally, the period of youth is separated from that of childhood by a threshold composed of a combination of school leaving and access to working life, which is crossed irreversibly, the accession to stable, permanent employment closes a period of transition of variable duration, with alternating spells of insecure employment, unemployment and training courses, and the lower the level of academic achievement, the longer this transitional period lasts.

Because they are deprived of the physical foundations of their independence ("No job, no wages, or odd jobs and low wages, that is the situation", writes C. Baudelot), [6] the form and the course of the normal process of release from family authority are modified.

Under the traditional model, residential dependence and all that goes with it were offset (and hence also limited) by the financial independence of the young wage-earner (in some cases, by the financial support provided to the family of origin) and the freedom he or she enjoyed by virtue of his/her position reflected this state of balance. The long-term lack of financial autonomy following the completion of schooling does not so much prolong the young person's stay in his family but modifies his status pending access to stable employment (an extension of the stay in the family is observed only in the case of unemployed, non-working males). The extension of unemployment, insecure employment or out-of-school training leads to a redefinition of the first phase of experience for young people who are unqualified or poorly qualified when they leave school: this phase is characterised by financial and residential dependence, a transitional status between schooling and employment, such as that of apprentice, temporary worker or trainee, or a "pre-employment" status such as that of the jobless, and the demand for the traditional freedoms of youth (pocket money and outings). As far as men are concerned, access to stable employment is deferred in most cases until after the period of military service which terminates this pre-employment phase. For most of them, the second phase remains that of stabilisation prior to settling down, usually as a result of marriage at the age of about 25 for men (22 for women). However, the recent increase in cohabitation is leading to a redefinition of the model of "setting up house" for some of these people: those for whom cohabitation before marriage is an intermediate phase between young adulthood and family life. [7]

Thus, the traditional definition (for which the lower limit has moved some years forward in the span of life) no longer represents merely one focal point in a range of definitions for which the other main focus is prolonged unemployment at the school leaving stage and the financial dependence to which it gives rise: between these two borderline cases are found a series of intermediate situations of relative dependence involving the sequence of training, insecure employment and unemployment. In many cases, the clear-cut line of demarcation between childhood and youth has been replaced by a blurred transition. Similarly, the rise in cohabitation frequently leads to the insertion of a transitional phase between unmarried life (within or outside the family of origin) and marriage, so that the traditional rite of passage is replaced by a gradual progression from one state to the other (as well as from youth to adulthood). The alternation (between school and firm) which is characteristic of the trainee's pattern of experience, places him midway between the student and the wage-earner; his wage level gives him an intermediate position between financial dependence and independence vis-à-vis the family of origin; while his status is half way between the constraints and freedoms of young workers and the prerogatives of students.

As regards young people with "devalued" school-leaving certificates, who break off their studies at the end of the secondary cycle of education or after a brief spell at university, they are no doubt more affected than others by "the discrepancy between aspirations and objective opportunities"[8] and show the greatest attachment to the defence of the nominal value of the certificate and the realisation of their academic hopes. Thus, one can point to the "delaying tactics" already analysed by G. Lapassade in 1957,[9] the different forms of resistance to downgrading,[10] the work of redefining aspirations, redeployment and re-schooling strategies, etc.[11] There then appears a transitional stage between school-leaving and access to stable employment: the stage of "post-adolescence" described by J C Chamboredon.[12]

C. Aspects of the condition of young adult immigrants

The study of the question of young immigrants and, more particularly, of the offences they commit, brings one face to face with a social problem with political and bureaucratic (that is staturory and administrative) overtones.[13] Any attempt at scientific investigation should therefore begin with an analysis of the issues, of the interests underlying the different procedures ("semi-scientific", "administrative", or "political"). Attention should, therefore, first be paid to the definition (nearly always an implicit one) of the actual category of young immigrants. From the beginning of the crisis (that is, from the second half of the 1970s), most of the European host countries first slowed down immigration (by authorising family reunion and nothing more) and then suspended it altogether. As a result, it is true to say that, at the present day, there are practically no "young immigrants" in the traditional host countries any longer. In fact, the term young immigrants is used (incorrectly) to refer to the category of children of immigrant parents.[14]

A study of the socio-demographic characteristics of families of immigrant origin (little or no formal schooling in the family, parents who are manual or unskilled workers, high birth rate, social and spatial segregation, etc,) makes it possible to account for the characteristics of the "second generation": particularly high rates of academic failure, unemployment and crime.[15] Are these rates higher than those applicable to young indigenous people with the same social background who have followed the same pattern of education? Allowing for the difficulties raised by the task of compiling reliable statistical data, there appears to be no substantial difference.[16] However, the cultural strains provoked by discrepancies between socialisation in the family and socialisation at school as well as between the aspirations assimilated by peer groups and those of the family of origin,[17] would no doubt be enough to account for the relatively greater frequency of academic failure. Assuming that it can be established that the recorded rates of delinquency among young people from immigrant families are higher than the rates for young people from comparable indigenous families who have followed a similar pattern of education and employment, this could be accounted for by the fact that, on the one hand, the more or less blatant racism to which they are prey explains their greater difficulties of vocational integration, while on the other hand, the specific social supervision to which they are subject explains the likelihood of their being over-represented in delinquency statistics.[18]

65

II.   CONDITIONS AND ASPIRATIONS OF YOUNG ADULTS

The analogies of condition implicit in their identical standing in the cycle of life (that is, the dual transition from family of origin to procreative family and from the educational system to the labour market) are fundamental to the aspirations or psychological characteristics peculiar to young adults.

A.   Youth and "indetermination"

Given the fact that this transition from an initial social position (determined by both the position of the family of origin and the educational status) to a future position, (determined by "definitive" vocational integration and matrimony) can no longer be defined by the starting point but is not yet definable by the point of arrival (which remains more or less potential), youth is a stage of indetermination: vocational and matrimonial indetermination which varies from one extremity to the other of the social spectrum and which diminishes with time. It is minimal when the future seems assured at the school-leaving stage, that is, when the volume and composition of accumulated resources are such that the range of vocational and matrimonial options is at this point severely restricted: for most of the young adults with whom we are concerned here, occupational advancement and/or a good marriage are unlikely at this stage. On the other hand, indetermination is greatest in those circumstances where the chances of promotion are equal to the chances of downgrading or in situations where the possession of some specific sort of capital (physical capital: good looks or physical strength) may - with a little luck - modify the foreseeable path through life by facilitating a good marriage or a sports or artistic career. However, regardless of whether the range of possibilities remains open in *de facto* terms or has already been almost fully closed, the fact is that indetermination - albeit provisional - is also characteristic of this sequence of the life-span in as much as the gradual withdrawal from the family of origin facilitates an escape, in practical and subjective terms, from the constraints which it imposes, without however creating the immediate obligation to submit to the constraints of a procreative family.

It would therefore be necessary to study the varied social freedoms to which boys and girls gradually gain access: after leaving school, after the first job, after military service, after the age of civil majority, etc. And it would also be necessary to study the various constraints progressively imposed by the transition from insecurity to stability and from stability to setting up house in the relationship of a couple (whether married or not), the birth of the first child, etc. This chronological sequence in the life-span may, in particular, be characterised by a state of relative economic "weightlessness" given, on the one hand, the continued assistance of the family of origin (which provides full or partial support for the young jobless person and which remains for a long time a possible refuge in the event of the failure of an experiment in living separately, juvenile cohabitation, etc.) and, on the other hand, the absence - albeit provisional - of the pressures imposed by the setting up of a new stable family unit (that is, one with a child or children). It is therefore possible to understand the specific structure of the young person's budget (the importance of outings and related expenditure), as well as the relative freedom enjoyed by young people on the labour market, freedom to take their time before finding a suitable job and thus to avoid downgrading, or to give up a job which is unsuitable, etc. Looked at from this angle, the period of youth - at least for men - remains what it was previously: a period of "liberty" and relative freedom from care ("life's holiday season"), of temporary release from the specific constraints (primarily of a family nature) imposed on adults; it is necessary to "take advantage of one's youth" before this interlude of relative freedom comes to an end. Most young people who hold "devalued" technical diplomas or have left school with no qualifications and are doomed to unemployment or to unskilled jobs reserved for "young factotums", no longer nurture any illusions about their future and have a realistic view of their situation. This temporary freedom without illusions could be contrasted with the more or less illusory indetermination of those who keep up their spirits by means of a "social bluff" ("I am not a petrol-pump attendant, I work as one"), thus enabling themselves to adjust to a future which is already irreversible.

B.   The "age of classifications": rebellion and adaptation

Temporarily indeterminate, unclassifiable, youth is also the age of classifications in as much as it can be described as the stage of life during which "novices/candidates" accede to the labour market and the marriage market, there to negotiate a position of employment and a matrimonial alliance. These classifications (those which they apply and those which are applied to them) are strictly dependent on the quantity and the different types of capital (cultural, educational, economic, social, symbolic, cosmetic, etc) possessed, acquired and/or inherited, present and/or potential. A study of the interrelationship between classifications and self-classifications (especially in the occupational field), between the positions (occupied) and the disposition (to occupy them) demonstrates that youth may be simultaneously the age of rebellion and the age of adaptation. The age of rebellion whenever a discrepancy emerges between the positions actually occupied as a result of the classifications applied to beginners and the positions anticipated, that is to say their own self-classification. Either the positions actually occupied, though nominally identical, do not correspond to expectations (reflecting an anterior situation); or the positions actually accessible to the holders of nominally identical school-leaving certificates are no longer the same as those previously available (inflation-devaluation of educational diplomas); or again the pretensions inherited from the family are too ambitious in relation to the actual availability of positions (given the educational diplomas obtained) or the pretensions acquired through education are incompatible with the subordinate posts offered by the holders of the positions demanded. All these discrepancies between aspirations and positions account for the different forms of struggle, individual or collective, aimed at adjusting the situation. First of all, there is the adaptation of jobs to aspirations: this involves various forms, both individual and collective, of resistance to downgrading which are made possible by a relative and provisional state of "economic weightlessness", and in this connection youth is seen as the period when it is necessary to find a place for oneself. If it is impossible to find positions adapted to people's aspirations, aspirations have to be adapted to the posts available, and the established correspondence between qualifications and posts must be mentally accepted. It is then a question of lowering one's sights, of becoming more reasonable, not insisting, "putting water in one's wine", as they say - in short of gaining maturity. The period of youth then comes to be seen as the the time of acclimatisation, the time needed to get rid of illusions.

When, on the contrary, the classifications applied to them correspond to their own self-classifications and their aspirations are in harmony with their jobs in advance, the social structures are perpetuated without incident: it is therefore understandable that young people may be by turns rebellious or apathetic, dissident or conformist, revolutionary or conservative.

While the rebellion and/or disenchantment peculiar to youth are more often than not accounted for by the discrepancy between their aspirations and the positions given to them when they come on to the labour market, these attitudes may also be dictated by the discrepancy between the different attributes attaching to them during this period of life. J.C. Chamboredon[19] has placed emphasis on the conflicts spawned by prolonged schooling and the extension of the period of access to stable employment, as a result of the prolonged stay in the family of origin and the constraints which this involves, on the one hand, and the onset of puberty, on the other. In fact, the aspiration for sexual emancipation was to be revealed as one of the key themes of the youth uprisings of the early 1970s and as one of the driving forces behind the ensuing social changes. Generally speaking, rebellion or mere uneasiness may be caused by disparities in the attributes peculiar to this stage of life, that is to say by the lack of harmony between the different timetables of access to maturity. The same is also true, no doubt, of the discrepancy between the precocious exercise of adult sexuality and the delayed access to economic independence. Lastly, this propensity for rebellion on the part of young people (in different forms and for various reasons) can no doubt only be understood in the light of the scope for irresolution characteristic of this transitional period of life.

C. The changes connected with recent developments: disillusionment and disenchantment

The spread of unemployment and the uncertainty of the jobs occupied by young people with few if any qualifications are responsible for a twofold disillusionment, a twofold disenchantment: with regard to the present and with regard to the future. As far as the present is concerned, the endemic lack of money prohibits access to the "recreational activities for young people", and prevents them from "taking advantage of their youth". With the passage of time, as hope dwindles of finding a job corresponding to the qualifications acquired, in the case of those who have such qualifications, as prolonged unemployment alternates with training courses or precarious "odd jobs" for young "factotums" without there appearing any prospect of stable vocational integration, with its implication of separate living arrangements, the achievement of independence vis-à-vis the family of origin and the "founding of a family", disenchantment and disillusionment give way to concern, anxiety, despair and "rage".[20] The disillusionment (commensurate with the illusion nurtured as to the value of an educational diploma) caused by the downgrading of those who have acquired a "guaranteed" trade by means of a "devalued" diploma, the disenchantment of those who attended school just long enough (as a result of extended compulsory schooling) to enable them to imbibe an ingenuous and unprofitable "cultural good will", the confusion of those with no diploma whatsoever, whose only resource is unfashionable physical strength and obsolete "masculine values", all these attitudes doubtless have no automatic consequences for the changing trends in recorded juvenile delinquency.[21]

But any analysis of the contemporary forms of deviant behaviour by young adults (suicide, alcoholism and the spread of drug addiction, on the one hand, delinquency in its infinite variety of forms, on the other) must necessarily take them into account.[22]

III. SOCIAL PERCEPTIONS OF THE "DANGEROUSNESS" OF YOUNG ADULTS

Any survey of the social image of young people from the standpoint of their "dangerousness" entails the following requirements:

- that those surveyed have already formed an opinion on the question: however, that opinion may exist only in an embryonic state or even be only an *ad hoc* and/or convenient reply improvised for the survey: "the opinion survey opinion";[23]

- that the publicly expressed opinion corresponds to the privately held opinion: however, whether this so-called "personal" opinion is based on the principle of representation (the point of view of the "experts" or again that of the majority revealed by the surveys) or on that of class morality and individual experience, it may be expressed but also euphemised, censured, misrepresented, according to the perceived degree of justification or licence for making it public;

- that those surveyed reply to the same question: in point of fact, assuming that it has a significance for all the persons surveyed and/or that they have already asked themselves the question, there is no reason to believe that the significance will be the same for all of them;

- lastly, that the replies may be aggregated, regardless of whether they are made in response to the same question or conform to the intimate (private) opinion of those surveyed, and regardless of whether the persons concerned have an opinion on the question asked.

It can no doubt be assumed - as is done implicitly by opinion surveys on the feeling of insecurity - that most of the persons surveyed have an opinion on the "dangerousness" of young people or are likely to improvise such an opinion in response to the questions of the interviewers, but nothing is known of how these perceptions are formed. Ordinary cognitive perceptions no doubt owe as much (and frequently more) to the scientific opinions popularised by the press and/or to traditional political perceptions as to any direct experience of the "dangerousness" of young people in the theatre of everyday social life. Moreover, these ordinary perceptions necessarily vary from one extreme to the other of the social spectrum,[24] because the tendencies to appropriate, criticise and challenge scientific perceptions and political perceptions, in the same way as the practical experiences of the dangerousness/harmlessness of youth, themselves vary from one social class to another. Consequently, the declared feeling of insecurity may be a non-committal one and signify either nothing at all or, at least, something different from what it purports to signify (an ethical orientation, a more or less precise political stance, a desire to conform to formal rules, an attitude of good will on the part of the person interviewed, a euphemised, watered down, simplified, caricatured, distorted or hard-boiled version of any particular political or scientific perception), just as it may express - in the forms laid down by the opinion survey - a diverse range of social experiences which are nevertheless memorable in various respects: vague fear inspired in the dominant classes by young working class people, apprehension of the "contamination" of their lineage felt by members of the middle classes forced to co-exist with the underclasses and, more particularly, with their youngest elements, specific fear of theft and/or unprovoked assault, fear of "seeing their children turn out badly" inspired in the working classes by the extension of unemployment, etc.

A. Ordinary perceptions and scientific perceptions of the "dangerousness" of youth

The ordinary perceptions of the "dangerousness" of youth are no doubt partly rooted in and/or reinforced by the "scientific" perceptions. Attention could thus be drawn to the importance attached since the end of the 19th century to puberty and adolescents ("dangerous" or "in danger") in the proliferation of "scientific" treatises on sex: those of "the medical field first, which dealt with 'nervous disorders'; then the psychiatric treatises which began to investigate the problem of 'excess' and later that of onanism (...) the etiology of mental illnesses", and it could be shown that these theories are important because they call for the adjustment of innumerable institutional mechanisms and because they ultimately cover the whole of the social space.[25] These "scientific" dissertations concern adolescence and puberty in general, but the "dangerous young people" in this case are middle class adolescents: danger of degeneration which the adolescent brings upon himself and to which he exposes the line of descent. It is true that psychoanalysis has today obtained a virtual monopoly of scientific doctrine concerning sex, completely supplanting the medico-psychiatric theories of the late 19th century concerning adolescence, and that psychoanalysis no longer treats adolescents as "dangerous", but possibly as "endangered". However, it would no doubt be possible to lay bare "the invisible threads" linking psychoanalysis to the past it has rejected and, consequently, "the long-range influence" exerted by the "scientific" perceptions of the late 19th century on contemporary perceptions.

At the same time, a "scientific" body of thought was elaborated in respect of juvenile delinquency. It would be necessary to review the discussions concerning "criminal responsibility" and the share of "heredity" and "environment", respectively, in the origins of crime, the disputes between supporters of "the theory of the born criminal" inspired by evolutionist theories (Lombroso) and supporters of the "theories of degeneration" of the French psychiatric school (from which G. Heuyer drew inspiration), between "the psychiatric criminological school" and the "sociological" school (that of Tarde and Lacassagne) which saw in "delinquent children the impure product of an environment which is itself delinquent",[26] and it would also be necessary to show the place accorded to adolescence and/or puberty in the various etiologies of crime devised since the end of the 19th century. Duprat[27] sees the adolescent as a sick person in the making. A "born vagabond", "incapable of resisting the urge to travel",[28] he has his own pathology, "hebephrenia", defined as "a need to act which generates disdain for any obstacle, any danger": "young offenders worry us. Vicious and criminal adolescents frighten us", writes Duprat. However, the adolescents referred to in this case are exclusively those from working class backgrounds: "that the conscripts of crime should be the sons of manual workers, recruited exclusively from the urban under-class, was for them such a manifest fact", writes A. Faure, "that they make only brief references to it in their works". These "scientific" and controversial perceptions, ranging from "the dangerousness of youth" to "endangered youth", together with the supporting theories and the operational concepts which serve as their currency, as it were ("discernment", "educability" etc.), have guided lawmakers, inspired methods of "treatment", formed generations of educators and, as a result, no doubt continue even today to explain in part the lay perceptions of the "dangerousness of youth".

B. Ordinary perceptions and political perceptions of the "dangerousness" of youth

The contemporary political perceptions of the youth phenomenon seem to oscillate back and forth. Eclipses alternate with reappearances, indifference with curiosity, silence with idle chatter: "There is something ritualistic about the periodic astonishment of adults in our society, when they become aware two or three times in the course of each generation that their society is also composed of young people", wrote J. Monod[29] shortly before May 1968. Moreover, these observations concern first one then the other extremity of the social spectrum, working class young people on one occasion, those from the dominant classes on another, or more specifically some of them: the fraction which has become visible and which these theories help to make visible. Indeed, each period has an archetype associated with it ("the teddy boy", "the leftist", the "hooligan", "the hippy" etc.), more or less inspired by the scientific or semi-scientific perceptions of youth and capable of serving as a focus for the social malaise and/or the feeling of insecurity. Thus, in the course of the 1960s, the "blouson-noir" in France and the "teddy boy" in England occupied the centre of the media/political stage. After 1968, they were succeeded by "the leftist student" and subsequently the "hippy" before they, too, in their turn, were relegated backstage. The "loubard" (hooligan), closely related to the "blouson-noir" or "teddy boy" of earlier years, then made his appearance in the second half of the 1970s; since then, attention has remained focused on the working class suburbs.

How are we to account for these fluctuations in the political interest aroused by young people and the feeling of insecurity they inspire? Do they reflect fluctuations in the "dangerousness" of youth or are they dictated by the recurring perception of an unceasing phenomenon? In the second case, the youth revolts (alternating between the university campuses and the suburbs) and the concern to which they give rise would be connected with long-range phenomena: on the one hand, the inflation/devaluation of educational diplomas and the perpetual disparities/realignments between diplomas and the jobs to which they give access would be responsible for the crisis brewing over the past twenty years, which is sometimes manifest, sometimes invisible; on the other hand, endemic delinquency connected with the traditional forms of sociability among young people from a working class environment (where they learn the values of masculinity and the conversion of the "anti-school culture" into a "workshop culture"[30]) has probably been aggravated over the last fifteen years or so by the effects of the crisis, the downgrading of young people with vocational training diplomas and the difficulties of integrating young people with no qualifications. In the first case, on the other hand, the changing political perceptions of youth would reflect not so much the fluctuations in political interest as the sporadic revolts by particular segments of the young population, variations in their "objective dangerousness" (as may be recorded by the statistics on juvenile delinquency) and in the feeling of insecurity which they inspire (as may be revealed by opinion surveys). In fact, it should no doubt be considered that there are elements of both continuity and change in the phenomenon and the perception of it and that, if the alteration of the phenomenon modifies the way in which it is perceived, the perceptions (and their own requirements for renewal) help to produce the transformation of the phenomenon perceived. Generally speaking, it can be assumed that the appearance of alarmist perceptions of youth in the political field signals a crisis in the reproduction of social structures (sometimes at one end of the social spectrum, sometimes at the other) and/or a change, a reorientation, a disruption of the categories of perception. The concept of "the reserve army of the proletariat" (that is, "unskilled jobless young people" in contemporary political jargon) which since the 19th century has underpinned the theory of the "dangerous working classes", alternates with the concept of "surplus intellectuals" which gives rise to the theory of "frustrated intellectuals".[31]

C. Everyday perceptions and everyday experiences of the "dangerousness" of youth

These political perceptions of young people are often partially connected with the scientific perceptions. Thus, whether the issue is one of surplus intellectuals or the over-supply of juvenile labour, the demographic data serve as a "scientific" (that is, "quantified") backdrop to political alarmism; from this point of view, the political exercise could be described as one of transforming quantitative data ("the rise of the young") into social allegories ("the juvenile peril"). On the other hand, however, it could be shown how much the "scientific" perceptions owe to the ethical/political inclinations of "scientists", and thus to political perceptions also. Similarly, attention could be drawn to the influence exerted on the ordinary perceptions of the "dangerousness of youth" by these political and/or scientific perceptions: it is possible that opinion surveys record only the popularised forms of the political and/or scientific stereotypes which they themselves help construct. However, short of considering that the declared feelings of insecurity inspired by young people are never anything more than an "opinion survey opinion", it has to be assumed that these alarmist political and/or scientific perceptions of youth are imbibed and appropriated (and consequently also translated, adapted and transformed) only to the extent that they reflect a commonplace experience of "the dangerousness of youth" in everyday social life. The study of the everyday experience of young people and the feeling of insecurity which they may inspire brings out the distinction between two types of situation: those where representatives of different generations enter into relations with one another in a socially homogeneous universe and those where representatives of different generations with different social backgrounds enter into conflict.

In the first case, it would be necessary to study, for example, the various types of relationship between family generations in working class communities. In cases where -as most frequently happens - working class parents have working class children, it would be possible to imagine a straightforwrd process of reproduction which would go forward smoothly. However, in view of the fact that the career prospects of manual

72

workers are doubtless seen primarily as the reverse of the negative career prospects which lead to social destitution, any challenge to the vocational integration of children when they leave school is no doubt seen by their parents as the ever present threat of a lapse into insecurity, poverty and humiliation (delinquency for boys, prostitution for girls and, nowadays, drug abuse for both sexes). It is therefore understandable that the extension of school life, on the one hand, together with the prolonged crisis and, more specifically, growing unemployment, insecurity and loss of occupational status, on the other, through their effects on the different patterns of vocational integration for young people from working class communities, should have initially aroused the anxiety and indignation of fathers with regard to sons or daughters accused of idleness or moral perversion. These accusations evoked the anger of young people upset by the lack of understanding of their parents.[32] It might also be possible, however, with the prolongation of the crisis, that parents, torn between public moral indignation and private understanding of the young people whom they censure publicly, have finally come to terms with new standards of integration and that there has been a revival of intergenerational solidarity within the family, with sympathy taking the place of the feeling of insecurity.

It would also be necessary to study what the commonplace perceptions of youth may owe to the experience of confrontation in everyday social life between representatives of different generations and social classes. While it is true that environmental separation of the different social categories is the rule and that their co-existence in physical space is more often than not explained by the temporary convergence of very different trajectories, these situations involving the physical co-existence of social categories normally found side by side only in statistical tables doubtless encourage the development of the feelings of insecurity inspired by young people. J.C. Chamboredon and M. Lemaire[33] have shown that the attitudes with regard to physical proximity vary according to whether it facilitates closer contacts with higher social classes or whether, on the contrary, it results in proximity to the lower classes, and it is the groups at the extremities of the social spectrum who criticise this situation most strongly because it forces them into an "unnatural" form of co-existence: those at the bottom of the social ladder, because they are perpetually exposed to stigmatisation and humiliation; those at the top of the social ladder, because they perceive proximity as a form of promiscuity. If working class young people are the centre of attention in this connection and their ostensible "dangerousness" is explicitly invoked to justify declared feelings of insecurity, it is for one thing because they provide a focus for all the grievances of lower middle class morality (in which education is no doubt the central value) against popular moral standards (which allow "the young to fend for themselves"[34]), for another because they constitute the largest and most visible group in urban centres, and the one least subject to supervision, and lastly because delinquency by gangs of urban youths (assault, theft, vandalism, etc.) is not just a figment of the imagination of frightened middle class people, nor is the feeling of insecurity solely the product of a collective psychosis.

CONCLUSIONS

The adoption of a policy of vocational integration is the most important precondition for any policy aimed at preventing delinquency among young adults who usually have few qualifications if any, are not subject to the supervision exercised by the school, are free from family control, condemned to unemployment and uncertainty of employment and, hence, not subject to the discipline of the workplace, and who face indefinite delays in their settlement into a job and into married life.

The vocational integration of young adult offenders presupposes the introduction of appropriate vocational training schemes leading to genuine employment.

In order to deter young people from embarking on a criminal career and to prevent minor and/or occasional delinquency from being transformed into professional delinquency, it is necessary:

- to limit the imposition of prison sentences without remission (which are known to be not only costly but also pernicious in their effects) to last resort circumstances and, in such exceptional cases, systematically to separate young adult offenders from seasoned offenders (special detention centres or separate prison wings);

- as far as possible, to impose only conditional sentences (suspended sentence, probation);

- as the imposition of fines is usually impracticable, to give preference on a general basis to alternative measures in lieu of unsuspended prison sentences.

The application of all these measures presupposes the extension and mobilisation of the social welfare professions and the redefinition of their role.

Notes

1. On this subject, see A. Desrosieres, L. Thevenot, *Les catégories socio-professionnelles* (The socio-occupational categories), Paris, Editions La Découverte, 1988.

2. A. Percheron, R. Remond (eds.), *Age et politique* (Age and policy-making), Paris, Ed. Economica, 1991.

3. L. Thevenot, "Une jeunesse difficile. Les fonctions sociales du flou et de la rigueur dans les classements (A difficult youth. The social functions of vagueness and exactitude in classifications). *Actes de la Recherche en Sciences Sociales*, No. 26-27, March-April 1979, pp. 3-18.

4. See in particular, E. H. Erikson, *Adolescence et crise. La quête de l'identité*, (Adoloscence and crisis. The quest for identity), Paris, Ed. Flammarion, 1972.

5. The historical and social variations in the definition of youth are indeed mirrored by different aspects of the main educational, occupational and family events.

6. C. Baudelot, "La jeunesse n'est plus ce qu'elle était. Les difficultés d'une description" (Youth is not what it used to be. The difficulties of a description), *Revue Economique*, Volume 39, No. 1, January 1988, pp. 189-224.

7. On this subject, see G. Mauger, C.F. Poliak, "De la cohabitation chez les jeunes de milieux populaires (1975-85)" (Cohabitation among young working class people (1975-85)), *Dialogue*, No. 92, second quarter 1986, pp 76-87.

8. See P. Bourdieu, "Classement, déclassement, reclassement" (Grading, downgrading, upgrading), *Actes de la Recherche en Sciences Sociales*, No. 24, November 1978, pp 2-22.

9. G. Lapassade, "Le passage des études à la profession. Les conduites d'ajournement" (The transition from schooling to occupational life. Delaying tactics), *L'Ecole des Parents*, No. 8, 1957-58, pp 12-17.

10. See G. Mauger, C. Fosse-Poliak, "Du gauchisme à la contre-culture" (From leftism to counter-culture), *Contradictions*, Brussels, No. 38, winter 1983-84, pp 39-62; G. Mauger, C. Fosse-Poliak, "Précaires créatifs et créativité précaire. Apprentissages de la précarité" (Creative insecurity and insecure creativity. Lessons in life on the breadline), *Chômage, marginalité et créativité*, University of Geneva, 1987.

11. See O. Galland, "Précarité et entrées dans la vie" (Insecurity and accession to adult life), *Revue Française de Sociologie*, XXV, No. 1, 1984, pp 49-66; "Formes et transformations de l'entrée dans la vie adulte" (Patterns and alterations in the process of accession to adult life), *Sociologie du Travail*, No. 1, 1985, pp 31-52.

12. J. C. Chamboredon, "Adolescence et post-adolescence: remarques sur les transformations récentes des limites et de la définition sociale de la jeunesse" (Adolescence and post-adolescence: observations on recent changes in the limits and social definition of youth), *Adolescence terminée, adolescence interminable*, Paris, PUF, 1986.

13. On this subject, see A. Sayad, *L'immigration ou les paradoxes de l'altérité* (Immigration or the paradoxes of otherness), Brussels, De Boeck-Wesmael sa, 1991; in particular "Qu'est-ce qu'un immigré?" (What is an immigrant?), pp 49-77 and "L'ordre de l'immigration entre l'ordre des nations" (The system of immigration in the context of the international order), pp 289-311.

14. The rival category of "young second generation immigrants" is also a misnomer: the generation fathered by an "immigrant" generation no longer comprises "immigrants".

15. On these questions, see for example H. Malewska-Peyre et al, *Crise d'identité et déviance chez les jeunes immigrés* (Identity crisis and deviant behaviour among young immigrants), Paris, La Documentation Française.

16. See for example, "Social reactions to juvenile delinquency among young people coming from migrant families", European Committee on Crime Problems, Strasbourg 1989, especially p. 74; in the same connection, see also A. Lahalle, "Délinquance des jeunes immigrés et politique institutionnelle" (Delinquency among young immigrants and institutional policy), in H. Malewska-Peyre, Crise d'identité et déviance chez les jeunes immigrés, op. cit., pp 347-388.

17. See A. Sayad, L'immigration, op. cit., in particular "Les enfants illégitimes" (Illegitimate children), pp 183-258.

18. See A. Lahalle, "Delinquance des jeunes immigrés et politique institutionnelle", op. cit.

19. J. C. Chamboredon, "Adolescence et post-adolescence", op. cit.

20. This expression is borrowed from F. Dubet, *La Galère. Jeunes en survie* (The Crucible. Young people getting by), Paris, Ed Fayard, 1989.

21. A quantified description can be found in the report prepared by J. Junger-Tas, "The young adult offender, some quantitive and qualitative data".

22. For a statistical approach to the interrelationship between crime and economic status, see "Economic crisis and crime", European Committee on crime problems, 1985; on the same theme, an annotated bibliography concerning Germany, the United Kingdom, Belgium and France will be found in "Chômage des jeunes, délinquence et environnement urbain. Recherche bibliographique, Programme de recherches et d'actions sur l'évolution du marché de l'emploi" (Youth unemployment, delinquency and urban environment. Bibliographical research, research and action programme on

developments in the labour market), ECSC - EEC - ECAS, Brussels, 1988. For an ethnographic approach, see, among our recent publications, G. Mauger, "Les bandes, le milieu et la bohême populaire" (Gangs, the underworld and working class bohemianism), *Cahiers du PIRTTEM-CNRS*, No 2, December 1990. On "gangs": G. Mauger, C. F. Poliak, "Les loubards" (Hooligans), *Actes de la recherche en sciences sociales*, No 50, November 1983, pp 49-67; G. Mauger, "Les bandes" (Gangs), in *L'Univers des Loisirs*, Paris, Letouzey et Ané, 1990; G. Mauger, C. F. Poliak, "La politique des bandes" (Gang policy), *Politix* No 14, 2nd quarter 1991. On "working class bohemianism" and drug addiction: G. Mauger, C. F. Poliak, "Le style baba" (The bohemian style), paper presented at the National Colloquy of the French Ethnological Society, "Classes d'âge et Sociétés de jeunesse" (Age groups and youth societies), Le Creusot, 30 May-1 June 1985; G. Mauger, C. F. Poliak, "Précaires créatifs et Créativité précaire" (Creative insecurity and insecure creativity), in *Chômage, marginalité et créativité*, op. cit; G. Mauger, "L'apparition et la diffusion de la consommation de drogues en France (1970-1980). Eléments pour une analyse sociologique" (The appearance and development of drug consumption in France (1970-1980). Elements for a sociological analysis), Brussels, *Contradictions*, No 40-41, 1984, pp 131-148.

23. The expression is borrowed from P. Champagne, *Faire l'opinion, Le nouveau jeu politique* (Providing opinions, the new political game), Paris, Ed de Minuit, 1990.

24. Everything suggest that they also vary (like the feeling of insecurity) according to sex. Firstly because the perceptions (scientific, political, ordinary) of young women inspire less fear than those of young men and secondly because women are no doubt more subject than men to the "feeling of insecurity" or, at least, to certain of its forms. The perception of "the dangerousness" of youth varies not only according to sex and social background but also, undoubtedly, according to age.

25. On this subject, see M. Foucault, *La volonté de savoir, Histoire de la sexualité* (The desire to know, History of sexuality), Volume 1, Paris, Ed. Gallimard, 1976.

26. A. Faure, "Enfance ouvrière, enfance coupable" (Working class childhood, delinquent childhood), *Les Révoltes Logiques*, No. 13, 1981, pp 13-35.

27. Duprat is the author of a typical book on the obsessive concerns of his day: *La criminalité dans l'adolescence. Causes, remèdes d'un mal social actuel* (Adolescent crime. Causes and cures of a current social evil), Paris, Alcan, 1909.

28. According to A. Faure, for all those who studied the origins of crime at the time, "all these childhood offences came from the same mould, beginning with the most dangerous one for the person concerned, vagrancy, the real ticket to the world of crime".

29. J. Monod, *Les barjots* (The loonies), Paris, Ed. Julliard, 1968.

30. P. Willis, "L'école des ouvriers" (The workers' school), *Actes de la recherche en sciences sociales*, No. 24, 1978, pp 50-61.

31. R. Chartier, "Espace social et imaginaire social: les intellectuels frustrés au XVIIe siècle" (Social space and social fantasy: frustrated intellectuals in the 17th century), *Annales ESC*, No. 2, 1982, pp 389-400.

32. M. Pialoux, "Jeunes sans avenir et travail intérimaire" (Young people with no prospects and interim work), *Actes de la Recherche en Sciences Sociales*, No. 26-27, 1979, pp. 19-47.

33. J. C. Chamboredon, M. Lemaire, "Proximité spatiale et distance sociale. Les grands ensembles et leur peuplement" (Physical proximity and social distance. Large housing estates and their population), *Revue française de sociologie*, XI, 1970, pp. 3-33.

34. J. C. Chamboredon and M. Lemaire note that "The conflicts between adults and young people are (...) frequently conflicts between middle class adults and working class youngsters" ("Proximité spatiale et distance sociale. Les grands ensembles et leur peuplement" (Spatial proximity and social distance. Large housing estates and their populated), op cit): the antipathy of young people to adults is most intense when the "natural" and instinctual inclinations of adolescents are compounded by the "barbarism" of the lower classes".

CURRENT LEGISLATION AS REGARDS YOUNG ADULT OFFENDERS

REPORT

by
Mr Frieder Dünkel,
Max Planck-Institute, Freiburg
(Germany)

1. Young adults in (juvenile) criminal law - overview (age groups, systems emphasising youth care or punishment)

Young adults are defined differently in the various European legal systems. Frequently, as in the case of Germany, France, Greece and the Netherlands, the term covers the 18-21 age group. Sometimes 16-17 year-olds are also included. In England and Wales, for example, there are special provisions governing 17-21 year-olds (18-21 year-olds under the Criminal Justice Act 1991); in Portugal, since 1983 there has been a uniform system of juvenile criminal law for 16-21 year-olds. The lower age limit for the application of adult criminal law is thus generally 21, but there are some exceptions, particularly with regard to the punishment of 18-25 year-olds, as in the case of the Swiss work training institution, or the execution of sentences, with the frequent special provisions in the prison system for specific young offenders' establishments with age limits of 23, 24 or 25.

The special treatment of young adults must be seen against the background of juvenile (criminal) law systems which emphasise either youth care or punishment.[1] It is justified by the desire for a flexible system providing, on the one hand, youth care measures to meet the educational requirements of juveniles and young persons and, on the other hand, the more punitive sanctions of adult criminal law in order to be able to deal with particularly serious offences or offences which are not typically juvenile (for example, under road traffic law). This places young adults on the borderline between the various systems of special law for juveniles in the strict sense and the system of adult criminal law.

2. Theoretical basis for the treatment of young adults as a separate category

The objectives of national legislation for young adults are closely bound up with basic thinking about the development of independent juvenile criminal law. On the basis of the realisation that a clear dividing line at age 16, 17 or 18 cannot be justified in terms of developmental psychology,[2] most European countries have come to the conclusion that the principle of "education **instead of** punishment" or refraining from the traditional punitive sanctions of adult criminal law, especially imprisonment, allows for more appropriate treatment of criminal offences by young adults.

The upward extension of juvenile criminal law to young adults can also be justified by the longer duration of education and the delayed entry into working life or foundation of a family.

However, the generally accepted borderline of age 21 for the application of adult criminal law seems at least questionable. By way of example, mention should be made of a reform commission (the "Anneveldt" Commission) in the Netherlands which suggested uniform juvenile criminal law up to the age of 25, on the grounds "that the youth sub-culture ceased to have an influence on young people at this age, when a decisive choice was made between social integration and a criminal career".[3]

Similar suggestions based on considerations of juvenile sociology in favour of uniform young offenders' legislation were made in Germany in the 1960s and 1970s, though - as in Holland - without any chance of being implemented.[4]

In any event, even in countries where young adults are procedurally not covered by juvenile criminal law, it is recognised that either particular educational measures or at least more lenient penalties than those provided for by adult criminal law are required. This is in line with the objectives originally pursued in the development of independent juvenile criminal law, namely **more favourable** treatment of juveniles in relation to adults[5] and more lenient criminal law measures, either by waiving the principle of compulsory prosecution in favour of the discretionary principle, or the reduction or waiving of criminal penalties, or increased requirements for the infliction of a prison sentence. Where young adults are not placed on the same footing as juveniles, the aim is nonetheless to scale down penalties by comparison with adults. In theoretical terms this results in playing down considerations of general deterrence in favour of individual preventive measures. Accordingly, considerations of general deterrence should no longer be taken into account in either conviction or sentence,[6] as for example in German juvenile criminal law, in the case of serious criminal offences punishable by youth custody (imprisonment on grounds of the seriousness of the offence, Section 17 (2), second alternative, JGG - Juvenile Courts Act).

In some countries there are major exceptions to the recommended approach of treating young adults more favourably than adults. For instance, in Belgium ordinary criminal law is applied to road traffic offenders aged 16-17, or in Holland to particularly serious criminal offences committed by the same age group (see Article 77c 1 of the Dutch Criminal Code). These exceptions are, however, of relatively minor importance in Europe, in contrast to the USA (see the so-called waiver provisions[7]).

3.   The inclusion of young adults in juvenile (criminal) law

As already mentioned, many countries allow for the possibility of trying young (18-21 year old) adults under juvenile criminal law. For instance, in the **Netherlands**, under Article 77 d of the Dutch Criminal Code, the specific sanctions of juvenile criminal law can be applied when this appears appropriate having regard to the personality of the offender.

In **France**, with the reduction of the age of majority to 18 in 1974, youth care measures ("protection judiciaire") at first no longer applied to young adults. However, the Decree of 18.2.1975 provided for the possibility (under Article 16*bis* of the Order of 2 February 1945) of applying youth care measures to 18-21 year-olds who were now of full age under civil law, but only on a voluntary basis (at the specific request of the offender) and for a limited period. The provisions in force before 1974 governing educational measures for young adults were rarely used in practice. Over the period 1974-1977 the number of young adults in prison more than doubled from 3,000 to just under 7,000.[8]

By contrast, practice in relation to the **German** juvenile law introduced in 1953 developed quite differently. Section 105 (1) 1 JGG provides for the application of juvenile criminal law to 18-21 year-old adults, if "an overall assessment of the offender's personality, taking into account environmental conditions, reveals that at the time of the offence his moral and intellectual development was that of a juvenile". Juvenile criminal law is also to be applied if the offence is to be regarded as a "juvenile misconduct" according to its nature, circumstances or motives (Section 105 (1) 2 JGG.) Procedurally, young adults are always dealt with by the juvenile courts, even if adult criminal law is applied (see Section 108 (1) JGG). In this case, particular leniency is provided for by comparison with over-21 year-olds (for example, fixed-term instead of life imprisonment, or preventive detention for particularly dangerous or habitual criminals, see Section 106 JGG).

While in 1965 only 37,8% of young adults were convicted under juvenile criminal law, the proportions had reversed by 1989: 64,2% convicted under JGG, but only 35,8% under ordinary criminal law.[9] The complete inclusion of young adults under juvenile criminal law, as called for in the 1970s, has thus largely been accepted in practice. However, in practice there are variations according to specific types of offence and according to region (see Figure 1). In the case of serious violence, sex and drug offences, young adults are dealt with under juvenile criminal law in over 90% and even almost 100% of cases (for example, robbery 1989: 97%; intentional homicide 98%). The reason is that under Section 18 (1) line 3 JGG the scale of sentences applicable to adults does not apply to juveniles - in particular, a judge may reduce the minimum sentence applicable. Only in the case of traffic offences (1989: 56%) and offences punishable under the Aliens Act (1989: 82%), are young adults for the most part dealt with under adult criminal law. In the case of road traffic offences, this is because it is possible to impose fines under summary proceedings without a trial (which would be necessary under juvenile criminal law).

The predominant application of juvenile criminal law to young adults in **Germany** has been favoured since 1958 by case law whereby, if there is any doubt as to whether the young adult was to be regarded at the time of the offence as a juvenile in terms of moral and intellectual maturity, the courts order juvenile criminal law to be applied.[10] The Federal Supreme Court repeatedly upheld this case law in the 1980s, supporting the approach adopted by the courts.[11] The courts implicitly assume that the application of juvenile criminal law is normally more favourable to the young adult. In the Federal Republic of Germany, this would appear not to be the case for all types of offence, however, as recent statistical surveys show.[12]

Constitutional misgivings may be raised by the regional differences in court practice regarding Section 105 JGG. A regional analysis by Pfeiffer showed wide variations ranging for example in Lower Saxony from 8% to 43%, and in Nordrhein-Westfalia from 9% to 73%, in the proportion of young adults convicted under ordinary criminal law.[13] The same observation applies at the level of the *Länder*. Figures for the year 1989 show 95% of young adults dealt with under juvenile criminal law in Schleswig-Holstein and Hamburg, as against 46% in Baden-Württemberg and 40% in Rheinland-Pfalz (see Figure 1). Overall, there is a **North-South gap**,[14] with the *Länder* in the north increasingly applying juvenile criminal law. This inequality is rightly regarded as constitutionally undesirable and a breach of equality before the law.[15]

Nothing is known so far about practice in the eastern *Länder* which have been reunited with the Federal Republic since October 1990. The provisions of the JGG apply almost without exception to the new *Länder*, but the separate juvenile court system which was abolished in the GDR in 1968 is in the process of being re-established.

Particular attention may be drawn to Chapter 31, paragraph 1 of the Swedish Criminal Code: in **Sweden**, young adults aged under 21 can, instead of the normal adult penalties provided for in the Criminal Code, be ordered to be "taken into special care", whereby the criminal courts relinquish jurisdiction and refer the case to the social welfare authorities, which take appropriate juvenile welfare measures.[16] Fairly frequent use is made of this possibility. The basic principle is that "in the event of special need for care, the criminal penalty to which the offender is liable must be subordinated to appropriate social welfare measures".[17] In 1985, the maximum age for youth welfare orders was raised from 20 to 21 years.[18]

4. Leniency towards young adults under ordinary criminal law

Examples of leniency towards young adults by comparison with adults are provided within the framework of ordinary criminal law in **England and Wales, Scotland, Greece, Italy, Spain, France, Austria, Switzerland and Scandinavia.**

In **England and Wales** young adults, that is to say, 17-21 year-olds (18-21 year-olds from October 1992, under the Criminal Justice Act 1991), unlike in Germany (see 3 above) are dealt with not by juvenile courts, but by ordinary criminal courts. However, the restrictions benefiting juveniles as regards the infliction of prison sentences also apply to young adults. Section 1, sub-section 4 of the Criminal Justice Act 1982 provided that youth custody is to be inflicted only if the juvenile is unable or unwilling to respond to non-custodial measures. Youth custody was also possible if it appeared necessary for the protection of the public or if required by the seriousness of the offence. The Criminal Justice Act 1988 further restricted Section 1, sub-section 4 of the 1982 Act by limiting imprisonment for under-21 year-olds to particularly serious cases in which adults would be sentenced to imprisonment.

A finding that the young offender will not respond to other punishment must be based on "a history of failing to respond to non-custodial penalties" and so cannot apply to offenders with only one or no previous convictions. Accordingly, first offenders can be sentenced to imprisonment only for particularly serious criminal offences (for example, homicide). In contrast to the considerable increase in recent years up to 1989 in the population in adult prisons, the occupation of juvenile establishments in England and Wales has fallen sharply since 1985.[19] This is partly due to the reform which reduced minimum sentences from 6 to 4 months and maximum sentences to some extent from two years to one year (youth custody in the case of 15-16 year-olds)[20] under the juvenile system. The absolute figures for prison sentences fell over the period 1981-1989 among juveniles by 70%, among young adults from 1985 by 37%.[21] This is partly due to demographic changes,[22] but also to changes in sentencing.[23] This is especially true of districts where so-called

84

intermediate treatment schemes were established. Since 1983 the Department of Health and Security (which is responsible for juvenile welfare) has funded 110 "alternative to custody and care" projects under its "intermediate treatment initiative", in a total of 62 districts (as at March 1986). In these districts the proportion of sentences to youth custody fell particularly sharply.[24] The Criminal Justice Act 1988 clearly also had a substantial effect. In 1989, 1 700 fewer juveniles and 5 600 fewer young adults were sentenced to imprisonment than in 1987 (= -41% to -25%).[25]

The reform proposals put forward in February 1990 (Crime, justice and protecting the public-White Paper) called for an extension of juvenile court jurisdiction to 17-year-olds. The previous maximum of 120 hours' community service for 16-year-olds was to be aligned with the maximum of 240 hours for young adults and full adults. Such measures confirm the trend towards making alternatives to imprisonment more "credible" and more acceptable to the courts by making the provisions more strict (for example, combining probation with community service).[26] It was also suggested that juvenile detention which had been uniform since 1988 (detention in a young offender institution, removing the previous distinction between detention centre and youth custody) should not exceed twelve months for 17-year-olds, as was already the case for 15-16 year-olds.[27] The Criminal Justice Act 1991, due to come into force in October 1992, has put these reform proposals into effect and will extend the jurisdiction of juvenile courts to 17 year-olds.

A development in youth care was introduced in **Scotland** in 1968 under the so-called "children's hearings" for children up to age 16, in exceptional cases up to 18, which take the form of a discussion, with an initial informal attempt at conflict resolution.[28] Also worth mentioning are the special provisions for 16-21 year-olds, convicted under ordinary criminal law (by adult courts). The law prohibits the infliction of prison sentences for this age group. The pre-1980 provision was the relatively imprecise (1-3 years) Borstal sentence. This was replaced by detention for a period to be determined by the court, not exceeding the appropriate sentence for over-20 year-olds. Otherwise, the general sentencing limits apply. For sentences between 28 days and four months, the sentence is to be served in a special detention centre, otherwise in a juvenile prison, where the offender can remain until reaching the age of 21, in exceptional cases 23.[29] As in the case of adults, early release is possible after serving one third of the sentence. Whereas for under-16 year-olds in Scotland the juvenile welfare approach predominates, for 16-21 year-olds the approach is based more on judicial proceedings with constitutional limits and safeguards.

In **Italy** there are few special provisions for young adults, who are tried by adult courts. However, there is a visible trend towards sparing young adults more from prison sentences. Whereas for juveniles the suspension of prison sentences of up to three years is possible and the same is true in the case of over-21 year-olds for sentences of up to two years, young adults occupy an intermediate position with a maximum sentence of two years and six months qualifying for suspension (see Article 163, Italian Criminal Code). Further special features are to be found in so-called referral to the social services on probation, a kind of probationary supervision after at least four weeks' observation in a detention centre (see Section 74 of Act No. 354/75).[30]

Spanish criminal law includes special provisions for 18-21 year-olds only in the execution of sentence (see 8), but not in sentencing. Only for 16-18 year-olds is leniency provided for under Article 9 (3) in conjunction with Article 65 of the Spanish Criminal Code, or replacement of the sentence by referral to a special correctional establishment (for an indefinite period). The latter is insignificant in practice.[31]

In **France** there are no special provisions as regards sentencing for young adults, other than the possibility of extending certain educational measures under the Order of 2 February 1945 (see 3 above). Reduced sentences only affect juveniles (up to the age of 18). Juveniles aged over 13 may receive criminal sentences, but these are subject to an attenuation on the grounds of minority ("excuse de minorité"), unless in the case of 16-18 year-olds this is refused by the court on specific grounds (Article 2 of the Order of 2 February 1945).[32] The 1990 draft reform of the 1945 Order recommended a significant reduction of custodial penalties, including detention pending trial, but only in respect of under-18 year-olds. It is worth noting, however, that imprisonment for 13-16 year-olds is in future to be limited to a maximum of five years for serious crimes (including certain physical injury offences, drug trafficking and aggravated theft) and for 16-18 year-olds to a maximum of three years (for less serious offences) or ten years (for serious crimes). Adult sentences are halved for 13-16 year-olds as a result of the attenuation on the grounds of minority.[33]

Similar possibilities for reducing sentences are available in **Greece** for 18-21 year-olds, for whom sentences are reduced by half.[34]

In **Switzerland**, however, Article 64 of the Criminal Code provides for only optional reduction of sentences for 18-21 year-olds, if they "were not yet fully aware" of the wrongfulness of their action. Until 1971 general reductions of sentence were available for this age group, but have now been restricted to offenders not wholly responsible for their actions, given their state of development. Case law recognises however that, contrary to the strict wording, leniency may be granted "where awareness was present but the ability to act accordingly was not yet fully developed"[35] (in relation to the special measures of the work education institution for young adults see 6 below).

In **Austria**, according to Article 34, No. 1 of the Criminal Code, commission of an offence within the age range 19-21 is grounds for leniency. According to Article 36 of the Criminal Code, life imprisonment is prohibited for young adults aged 19 (as also for 14-19 year-olds, see Section 5 No. 2 Austrian JGG).[36]

Other possibilities for leniency are available in the **Scandinavian countries**, which have no separate juvenile criminal law and where in extreme cases prison sentences can be inflicted according to the ordinary Criminal Code. However, in **Denmark, Norway and Sweden**, a general provision for leniency on behalf of 15-21 year-olds allows the court discretion to inflict custodial sentences or fines, where in principle only custodial sentences are provided for.[37]

In some cases, as in **Denmark**, extensive forms of diversion (discharge) are available. In **Sweden** infliction of prison sentences was very considerably restricted in

86

1980 after the abolition of youth custody which had been relatively poorly defined (1-3 years). Consequently, for 15-18 year-olds, prison sentences may be inflicted only if there are "substantial" grounds, which appears to be the case in just under 1% of convictions. For 18-21 year-olds, the ultima ratio principle of imprisonment is more strictly observed, in that "special" grounds are required in relation to general compliance with the Law.[38] Whereas sentencing for over-21 year-olds entails imprisonment in virtually one case in four, the proportion for young adults is only about 10%.[39]

A further peculiarity concerns suspension of sentence combined with probation in **Finland**. For 15-21 year-olds prison sentences of up to two years may be suspended subject to probation, including cases where this would not be possible for over-21 year-olds because of previous offences.[40]

Furthermore, under new legislation which came into force in 1990 - similar to the situation in Sweden - infliction of prison sentences on 15-18 year-olds is confined to cases where "serious" grounds make it necessary.[41]

All in all, there is a general trend **all over Europe** towards giving young adults more lenient treatment than over-21 year-olds, in so far as they are not covered anyway by the more lenient juvenile criminal law, and towards not applying punitive sanctions.[42] Further possibilities to exercise discretion (not to sentence or not to prosecute, diversion etc.), the further development of alternatives while diminishing the use of imprisonment according to the ultima ratio principle, constitute the main lines of a crime policy, applying also to young adults, which takes more fully into account both the development-related nature of juvenile delinquency (episodic character, spontaneous reform with increasing maturity) and the possible negative consequences of formal state intervention (stigmatisation).

5.   **Removal of young adults from the scope of (juvenile) criminal law and their trial under adult criminal law**

The general tendency towards leniency for young adults in (juvenile) criminal law matters contrasts with instances in which juveniles and young adults are transferred within the scope of adult criminal law. The most extreme example is no doubt the USA, where in the last 15 years there has been an about-turn in crime policy, with emphasis on deterrence and incapacitation, leading to further removal of young adult offenders from the scope of juvenile criminal law. The increasing use of so-called "waiver" judgments corresponds to a development in crime policy which, on the one hand, seeks to treat status offenders more leniently through diversion measures (especially avoiding imprisonment), while on the other hand allowing for transfer under the jurisdiction of adult courts and hence full criminal responsibility in most states from the age of 13-16 (in some cases with no legally fixed lower limit).[43] In extreme cases, this opens up the possibility of sentencing young adults to the death penalty.

In recent years there has been an increase in transfers to adult courts, even legally removing any limitation in respect of specific types of offences, such as the most serious crimes.[44]

There are scarcely any similar provisions in **West European countries**. However, in **England** a sentence of life imprisonment for murder is possible for 18-21 year-olds[45]. In the **Netherlands** in exceptional cases 16-18 year-olds can be punished according to adult criminal law, which is possible in **Belgium** only for traffic offenders.[46] In the latter case, as in Germany (see 3 above), it is not a question of wishing to impose stricter penalties, but rather of using the possibility under adult criminal law of inflicting fines (in summary proceedings) without holding a full trial. In the **Netherlands**, 16-18 year-old traffic offenders are also often sentenced under adult criminal law, because only by this means is disqualification from driving available as an additional penalty.[47]

Apart from road traffic offences, the juvenile courts can refer the offender to the ordinary courts in **Belgium** also in cases where the specific penalties provided for by the Youth Protection Act (Section 38) do not appear appropriate.

Overall, in European countries the possibilities for removing juveniles from the juvenile criminal law system and sentencing them according to adult criminal law remain both statutorily and practically the exception. This is, in practice, also the case with corresponding flexible provisions for young adults such as they exist in Germany (see 3 above).

6. Specific sanctions for young adults

In general, young adults are subject either to the specific provisions of juvenile criminal law or youth welfare law, or to reduced penalties under adult criminal law.

In this connection, a number of innovations in German criminal law should be mentioned, which also generally apply to young adults (see 3 above). The 1990 reform both expanded diversion provisions and systematically gave priority to the dismissal of proceedings in trivial cases, where educative measures (specifically placed on a par with attempts to make amends or redress the damage caused by the offence) are put in hand or completed. This confirms the "juvenile criminal law reform through practice"[48] developed in the 1980s and found positive. The proportion of proceedings dropped under Sections 45 and 47 JGG (that is, by the prosecution or the court, possibly in combination with community service orders, forms of care involving probation, etc.) rose from 43% in 1980 to 56% in 1989.[49] The reform also broadened the range of sanctions to include the hitherto experimental "new non-custodial measures":[50] community service (also as so-called disciplinary measures[51]), care orders, social training courses[52] and mediation between the offender and the victim.[53] The possibilities for suspending youth custody sentences of 1-2 years were also expanded (see Section 21 (22) JGG), thus confirming a development which had been anticipated in practice (in 1989, despite restrictive statutory conditions, 51% of such juvenile sentences were suspended)[54] and in case law. The expansion of these alternatives, applied also to young adults, together with a slight decrease in crime and a small demographically determined fall in the number of cases, contributed to a 40% lower population in juvenile detention centres over the period 1983-90.[55] More than 90% of the juvenile prison population in Germany is made up of young adults (under 25).[56]

An important **special provision** is to be found in **Swiss** criminal law. Under Article 100 *bis* No. 1 of the Swiss Criminal Code an **18-25 year-old**, whose psychological development is substantially disturbed or endangered, who is "wayward, dissolute or work-shy" and whose offence is related to those circumstances may be committed to a **work education institution** instead of being sentenced, if this would appear a more effective preventive measure. In the institution, the offender is trained to work and his occupational knowledge is to be furthered (Article 100 *bis* No. 3 Swiss Criminal Code). Detention in such an institution lasts at least one year and not more than three years (see Article 100 *ter* No. 1 and No. 2 Swiss Criminal Code). In exceptional cases, the measure may be extended for not more than one year. In the event of early conditional release the offender is placed on probation for 1-3 years.[57]

The theoretical basis for creating a separate category of young adults aged 18-25 lies in the special exposure to crime of this age group, which accounts for one-quarter of convictions under the Criminal Code and in which personality development is basically not yet complete, offering a good chance of educational measures being effective.[58] Sentencing practice seems somewhat reserved, which may be due not least to the high minimum period of referral of one year.[59] Moreover, capacity is relatively limited: in total four institutions with some 200 places.[60] Although staffing provision in these institutions, which sometimes offer socio-therapeutic programmes such as in the Arxhof Institution until 1988, seems to be better than in most adult prisons, statistics for further offences do not demonstrate any obvious superiority of this type of institution for preventive purposes.[61]

The Portuguese legislator also stated the importance of education as a reason for the separate "young adults criminal law" introduced in 1982.[62] The age of criminal responsibility in **Portugal** (as in Spain) is 16. The new legislation applies to 16-21 year-olds and provides for specific juvenile sanctions ("correctional measures"): warning, imposition of special duties, fines or detention of between three and six months.[63] The correctional measures are intended to replace custodial sentences of up to two years. In any event, custodial sentences for 16-21 year-olds are to be made more lenient[64] and served in special juvenile detention centres.[65]

For under-18 year-olds conventional protection measures (for example, educational supervision, placement in foster families, placement in homes, etc.) may be applied.

7. Sentencing practice regarding young adults by comparison with juveniles older adults

The fact that young adults, by comparison with juveniles, more frequently receive custodial sentences and longer sentences is not surprising in view of the nature of their offences. Among young adults, the more serious forms of property crime, including robbery, are much more significant than among juveniles. Accordingly, for example in **Germany** in 1989 9,5% of juveniles but 20,2% of young adults were sentenced to youth custody (the proportions of youth custody without suspension were similar: 3,0% for juveniles, 7,6% for young adults).[66]

89

For these reasons it is also to be expected that more use will be made for juveniles than for young adults of the possibilities of diversion, owing to the triviality of most juvenile crime. In **England and Wales** in 1989, 50% of male 10-14 year-olds, 29% of 14-17 year-olds, but only 12% of 17-21 year-olds convicted were discharged (absolute or conditional discharge). However, as in the case of children and adolescents, the proportion among young adults (6%) has doubled since 1979.[67] In the **Netherlands**, owing to the prevailing principle of discretionary prosecution, diversion is particularly frequent. Just under 80% of juvenile delinquency proceedings recorded with the prosecution authorities end in a discontinuation of proceedings.[68] However since the relevant guidelines were issued by the prosecution service in 1985 a tendency may be observed towards fewer cases of discontinuation of proceedings (on grounds of triviality), in favour of conditional discharge combined with special duties (for example, payment of a fine along the lines of the so-called "transaction" procedure).[69] Unfortunately, data for the practice concerning young adults are not available. In the Scandinavian countries, which have no separate juvenile criminal law, but some extended provisions governing diversion and only restricted use of custodial sentences, sentencing practice concerning 15-18 year-olds is especially lenient and for 18-21 year-olds somewhat lenient. For instance, in **Denmark** two-thirds and in **Finland** one-third of proceedings against juveniles are dropped, whereas such cases are exceptional for young adults.[70] In **Sweden** some 70% of proceedings against juveniles but only 20% of proceedings against young adults are discontinued.[71] In addition, a substantial proportion of juveniles are referred to the youth welfare authorities (see 3 above).

The new **Austrian** JGG in force since 1 January 1989 has led to thorough changes in sentencing practice. While the previous legislation offered virtually no possibilities of discontinuation of proceedings by the prosecution,[72] the 1989 Reform Act opened up extensive extrajudicial forms of proceedings, especially in combination with mediation between the offender and the victim or reparation (see Sections 6 and 7 JGG). In the first years after the entry into force of the Act (1989 and 1990), no fewer than 72,8% of all proceedings against juveniles up to 19 years of age were discontinued, most (54,4%) without any penalty, 8,1% in conjunction with mediation between offender and victim.[73] In the other cases, only a conviction without penalty ("Schuldspruch ohne Strafe" under Section 12 JGG) (1,8%) or a conviction with deferment of sentence ("Schuldspruch unter Vorbehalt der Strafe" under Section 13 JGG) (6,9%) were given, leading to a rate of juvenile sentencing of only 19,1% to the conventional punishments of fines and custodial sentences, whether suspended or otherwise. The conviction rate for young offenders recorded by the police decreased from 27% in 1988 to 19% in 1990 despite the inclusion of 18 year-olds.[74] Regarding the possibility, introduced by the Criminal Law Amendment Act of 1987, of discontinuation of proceedings by the prosecution under Article 42 of the Criminal Code, no differentiated sentencing data are yet available for over-19 year-olds.

In **Germany**, there are few differentiated data on diversion practice comparing juveniles and young adults. The proportion of discontinued proceedings through the exercise of discretion have increased - as already mentioned - to 56% (1989) (see 6 above). A representative survey by Heinz and Hügel did show that proceedings against 14-17 year-olds were more frequently dropped than against 17-20 year-olds, but the differences largely disappear when the variable of previous offences is taken into account. With only **one** previous entry in the register, 51,4% of juveniles and 48,9% of young adults were convicted.[75] The higher rate of discontinuation of proceedings among juveniles is accordingly explained primarily by their usually less extensive previous record.

Considerable importance for crime policy attaches, however, to sentencing practice in relation to young adults as compared with over-21 year-olds. In 1988 a report laid before parliament in **England** ("Punishment, custody and the community") found that the courts inflicted custodial sentences more frequently on the 17-20 age-group than on the over-21 year-old age group.[76] Attention was also drawn to the sharp contrast in sentencing practice as between 16 year-olds and 17 year-olds. Almost twice as many 17 year-olds as 16 year-olds were given custodial sentences, a difference which could be explained to only a small extent by differences in the seriousness of the offences or of the offender's previous record. Consequently, it was recommended, particularly for 17-20 year-olds, to develop community-based programmes in combination with community service, so-called day training centres, and probationary services in general.[77] In the 1990 Home Office White Paper and the Criminal Justice Act 1991 these findings are taken into account in so far as 17 year-olds are now to be included in the juvenile courts system and so placed on the same footing as 16 year-olds and younger offenders with regard to penalties and sentencing.[78]

Similar results were produced by several surveys (using statistical analysis) in **Germany**. The starting-point for comparative analysis of sentencing practice is favourable in Germany in so far as young adults can be dealt with under juvenile or adult criminal law according to their degree of maturity (see Section 105 JGG and 3 above). However, it must be remembered that the treatment of young adults under juvenile law varies considerably in practice according to the type of offence and between regions (see 3 above). In a comprehensive statistical analysis using comparable groups of offences, Dünkel carried out an investigation into young adults convicted under juvenile law in comparison with those convicted under adult criminal law. With the exception of robbery and homicide, it emerged that young adults convicted under juvenile law were considerably more frequently sentenced to youth custody without suspension.[79] For theft offences, the figures were 12% as against 4%, for sexual offences 29% to 20% and for other offences against the person 9% to 2%. For robbery 43% of young adult offenders convicted under JGG were immediately taken into custody, as compared with 51% of those convicted under adult criminal law.

If we consider these categories of offences in relation to the length of custodial sentence, substantially more young adults were sentenced to short terms of up to one year under adult criminal law, which provides for custodial sentences of less than six months.

In German juvenile criminal law, under Section 18, sub-section 1 JGG, the minimum sentence is fixed at six months, whereas for adults (though since the Reform of 1969 only in exceptional cases, see Article 47 of the Criminal Code) sentences of between one month and six months are also possible. Only for robbery was a similarity in the length of sentences to be observed, though with comparatively more sentences in the range above 3 to 5 years upon conviction under adult criminal law. This is explained by the specific penalties provided for under the stricter adult criminal law, which do not apply under juvenile law (see Section 18, sub-section 1 (3) JGG). In the case of robbery and other particularly serious criminal offences it may be assumed that young adults are dealt with increasingly under juvenile law in order to avoid these high minimum penalties.

Summarising, Dünkel observed that, with the exception of convictions for robbery and homicide, under juvenile law convicted young adults run a higher risk of receiving a custodial sentence, or receiving a longer sentence, than if they are dealt with under adult criminal law.[80]

Similar results were arrived at by Pfeiffer in a study carried out in three *Länder* (Niedersachsen, Hessen and Saarland), based on an examination of individual groups of offences, particularly taking account of offenders' previous records. Twenty-year-olds sentenced under juvenile law were compared with 21-year-olds sentenced under ordinary law. He found that the proportion of under-20 year-olds given custodial sentences without suspension was 2-3 times higher than among older offenders. Further differentiation according to the seriousness of the offences produced the same results as were arrived at in Dünkel's survey, namely that as the seriousness of the offence increases, so the sentence under adult criminal law is more severe. Pfeiffer summed up this finding as follows: "If prominence is given at the trial of a previous offender for a minor-to-moderate offence to the fact that he is to be convicted again, there is a higher risk for under-21 year-olds of being given a youth custody/prison sentence without suspension. If, however, greater emphasis is placed on the offence itself because of its seriousness, there is greater probability for the adult previous offender of receiving a prison sentence without suspension.[81]

A wider investigation carried out by Pfeiffer in all the *Länder* of the former Federal Republic of Germany into the practice from 1984-1989 in respect of the 14-21 and over-21 age groups provided striking confirmation of the results mentioned. Even with only one previous conviction 14-21 year-olds run a greater risk of being detained pending trial and receiving a custodial sentence than over-21 year-olds. A comparison of 21 year-olds with 20 year-olds proved the existence of discrimination in the juvenile courts even taking account of their previous convictions and the offences. Discrimination against adults was apparent only in respect of serious offences such as homicide, rape or robbery.[82]

All in all, there is a striking, surprising **tendency to sentence young adults more heavily under juvenile criminal law** - at least as regards the application of youth custody/imprisonment - though further empirical analysis is necessary. Dünkel found in his investigation that the increasing treatment of young adults under juvenile criminal law had raised new problems. In order to avoid placing young adults at a greater disadvantage, he calls for reform of the law in order to circumscribe the conditions for sentencing to youth custody more strictly and abandonment of the concept of "harmful tendencies" as a justification.[83] In fact here it is a question of greater severity on the grounds of previous offences, which the legislator abandoned in adult criminal law as long ago as 1986. Also several writers are calling for stricter adherence to the principle of proportionality ("Tatproportionalität") and proof that the measure (that is, youth custody) is appropriate and necessary (in the sense of special prevention) taking into account the alternative penalties.[84] The call for abolition of youth custody on grounds of harmful tendencies, which is justified in case law by the need for longer general education, by a special education requirement,[85] is now supported by a very large majority of scholars and professionals.[86] The German legislator was called upon by a resolution of the Bundestag in June 1990 to overhaul the conditions for sentencing to youth custody, as part of the overall reform of German juvenile criminal law now under way, by October 1992.[87]

8. Young adults in detention pending trial

The practice of detaining juveniles and young adults pending trial is regarded internationally as a special problem.[88] There are some indications that - although no additional grounds for detention are specified by law for this age-group - detention pending trial is ordered more frequently than for over-21 year-olds. For example, the ratio of prisoners on remand to prisoners serving sentences in Germany among over-21 year-olds is approximately 1:4, but among 18-21 year-olds it is 1:2 and among juveniles only 1:1.[89] About half of those detained pending trial are not given an unsuspended custodial sentence.[90] In many cases, therefore, detention pending trial takes over the function of a short custodial sentence-although this was in principle abolished by the legislator (see Article 47 of the Criminal Code and Section 18 JGG, whereby the minimum youth custody sentence is six months). Empirical investigations have shown that, especially for juveniles and young adults, unlawful ("apocryphal") grounds for detention come into play.[91]

In international discussion on reform emphasis is chiefly placed on the avoidance of detention pending trial for juveniles, but the relevant programmes or reforms sometimes also include young adults. The 1990 Reform of the JGG in Germany restricted to juveniles the direct involvement of social workers in the juvenile courts (for investigation of the offender's social and personal situation[92]) and the mandatory appointment of counsel (see Section 72a and Section 68 No. 4 JGG), but this social service (known as "detention decision" assistance) is also involved in proceedings against young adults and is required to report promptly in cases involving detention (see Section 107 and Section 38 (2) JGG). Particular shortcomings are observed in international comparisons in the execution of detention pending trial. Frequently, the general requirement of separation from adult detainees or prisoners serving sentence is not observed. Conditions of detention are often worse than in prison, because there is a lack of staff and of facilities (for appropriate recreation, regular visits, etc.).[93] Apart from programmes to avoid or shorten detention pending trial, such as are being experimented with in **England, France and the Netherlands**, greater importance is being attached to ways of making sensible use of the time spent in detention pending trial. In this connection, particular attention may be drawn to the **Austrian** JGG of 1989 which (for up to 19 year-olds) makes possible the provisional voluntary execution of sentence following a finding of guilt at first instance, if a custodial sentence is to be expected (see Section 36, sub-section 2, JGG). A similar (general) provision exists in **Switzerland** and is frequently applied.[94] Provisional commencement of sentence makes it possible, for example, for the offender to be catered for more quickly in educational or vocational training schemes. However, because of the presumption of innocence, the consent of the prisoner to a provisional commencement of sentence is an absolute requirement. In **Germany**, for young adults up to 21 years of age educational provision must be made during detention pending trial (see Section 110, sub-section 2 and Section 93 JGG). The 1990 Reform Act extended the scope of this provision to up-to-24 year-olds. It remains disputed whether, in addition to educational **facilities**, educationally motivated **impositions,** such as the compulsory work advocated for juveniles (widely regarded as unconstitutional[95]), are also possible.

Efforts to reduce detention pending trial for juveniles and young adults have been successful in some countries in recent years. For instance, violent criticism in the mass media and by scholars in **Germany** has brought about a reduction in figures for detention pending trial over the period 1983-1989 of 56% among juveniles and 46% among young adults.[96] In **France**, detention pending trial for minor offences was abolished for under-16 year-olds in 1989. The number of corresponding prisoners detained pending trial fell from 1 411 in 1981 to 170 after the Act came into force in 1989. The figure for 16-18 year-olds in detention pending trial also fell steeply between 1981 and 1989, from 4 642 to 2 102.[97] A current bill dating from 1990 seeks to restrict detention pending trial for 16-18 year-olds[98] even further. In **England** the detention pending trial figures fell for the first time in 1989; this is partially attributed to custody avoidance programmes and alternative accommodation facilities.[99] Future crime policy should increasingly include young adults in efforts to improve the situation in detention pending trial and to avoid the imprisonment of juveniles.

9. Special provisions governing the prison treatment of young adults

Even in countries where little or no special provision is made as regards young adults in criminal law, distinctions are made for this age group by comparison with adults in relation to the prison system. A typical example is **Spain**, where - as previously stated - there are no special provisions for 18-21 year-olds in the Criminal Code. However, the Spanish Prison Act provides - like the corresponding Act in **Portugal** (see 6 above) - for the detention of 16-21 year-olds, and in special cases even up to 25 year-olds (see Section 9 No. 2 of the Prison Act), in special institutions. The same applies to detention pending trial (see Section 8 No. 3 Prison Act).

A separate section of the prison regulations deals with execution of sentence in juvenile prisons. Special emphasis is placed on education through pedagogical and psychological measures which are as far as possible adapted to the situation outside prison.

Juvenile prisons are required to be better equipped than adult prisons as regards both premises and staff. Clause 52 of the prison regulations stipulates the provision of small units for 20 to 30 prisoners. In addition the staff are supposed to be specially trained. Juvenile detention is designed to be conducted in stages with special concessions with regard to possessions and relaxation of restrictions (regarding recreation, passes, leave, etc.).[100] Practice seems, however, to fall far short of the theory: there are still old buildings where there is no separation of remand prisoners

94

and those serving sentences and where conditions do not always differ to the desired extent from those of adult prisoners.[101]

In other countries too - where there is no juvenile detention in the strict sense (in **Germany**, for example, 18-25 year-olds account for 90%[102]) - distinctions are made within the adult prison system with regard to young offender institutions in which up-to-25 year-olds are held.

Within the juvenile prison system there are often provisions enabling offenders to remain in the relevant institutions after reaching the upper age-limit of 21, where this is judged appropriate on educational grounds (see, for example, provisions in **Germany, Austria** and **Portugal**). Corresponding age-related distinctions are less marked in the **Scandinavian countries**, because there priority is given to the principle of detention close to the offender's home.[103] However, there are individual so-called young offenders' institutions such as Ringe in **Denmark** (as a rule for up-to-23 year-olds) within the system of closed prisons for inmates serving long sentences.[104]

10. Reform trends in the treatment of young adults in (juvenile) criminal law

Regarding the treatment of young adults under (juvenile) criminal law, no uniform trends can as yet be identified in the western European countries. However, there are **efforts**, to enable **young adults** to benefit more from the **theoretically more lenient juvenile criminal law**. This is particularly so in **Germany**, where the call to deal with young adults entirely under juvenile criminal law has enjoyed a general consensus since the mid-1970s and will presumably be translated into law with the overall reform of juvenile criminal law which is to be drafted by 1992. In this connection however, attention should be drawn to the possibly less advantageous position of young adults revealed by empirical investigations. To that extent, the extension of juvenile law to young adults might be regarded as a backward step, unless the whole of juvenile criminal law is made more clearly subject to constitutional safeguards, with further development of the idea of sentence's proportionality to the offence. Consequently in **Germany**, for example, a drastic reduction in youth custody sentences (at present 6 months to 5 years; for young adults up to 10 years) to 1 month / 2 to 5 years is advocated.[105]

A first step towards complete coverage of young adults under juvenile criminal law was taken by the **Austrian** legislator with the JGG reform which came into force at the beginning of 1989. The scope of juvenile law was extended to the age of 19. Consequently the newly-introduced possibilities of decriminalisation in connection with so-called conflict resolution (mediation/reparation, etc.) also apply for up-to-19 year-olds, together with the possibility of suspension of sentence with probation, irrespective now of the length of sentence.[106]

Irrespective of the legal framework for dealing with young adult offenders in future, it would seem necessary to provide for some degree of flexibility. This should allow both for developmental difficulties by means of specific educational rather than punitive measures; at the same time educational sanctions, however well-meant, should never be out of proportion to the offence and should therefore also be subject to

constitutional safeguards, having due regard to proportionality. It must be added that the need for preservation applies not only to safeguards in respect of sentencing or other sanctions but also to procedural safeguards such as the right to defence counsel, the right of appeal, etc. The **guidelines** for **reform** of **criminal law** in relation to **young adults** should be to **afford more favourable treatment** and to impose **more lenient sentences by comparison with adults**, and to apply constructive penalties.

If in Europe we wish to follow the course for crime policy laid down by the Beijing rules and the laws of most countries which have specific independent juvenile courts, it may prove essential to include 18-21 year-olds in these, especially since as a result of demographic changes and the drop in the crime rate such specialised legal services for under-18 year-olds will no longer be justifiable from a quantitative point of view. This means that it will be difficult to maintain the juvenile courts unless their jurisdiction is extended.

Lastly it should be emphasised that it is only possible and desirable to include young adults within a system of law (offering safeguards of fundamental rights) and not within a system of youth care.

Notes

1. For a description of the different approaches see <u>Kaiser</u> 1985, 441;
<u>Dünkel</u> 1989, 130 et seq.; 509 et seq.

2. <u>Meschler</u>1985, 107 argues on developmental psychology grounds for subjecting young adults on principle to juvenile criminal law, since developmental forces are still extensively effective in any person aged under 21.

3. see <u>Scholten and ten Siethoff</u> 1985, 650.

4. see for example, <u>Asbrock</u> 1977, 191 et seq.; <u>Kaiser</u> 1977, 51 et seq. with further references.

5. see <u>Pieplow</u> 1989; Heinz 1991.

6. see <u>Eisenberg</u> 1991, marginal reference 5 relating to paragraph 17; <u>Dünkel</u> 1990, 20 et seq. with further references.

7. see, summarising, <u>Feld</u>, 1987, 505 et seq.

8. see <u>Ministère de la Justice</u> (ed): "Protection judiciaire de la jeunesse". Conseil du Ministre 17 May 1989, 7.

9. see <u>Statistisches Bundesamt Wiesbaden</u> (ed): Rechtspflege. Reihe 3. Strafverfolgung 1989, Wiesbaden 1990, 15 et seq.; on development up to 1987 see <u>Dünkel</u> 1990, 87 et seq., 710.

10. see BGHSt 12, 116 et seq.; BGHStV 1989, 311 et seq.

11. see BGHStV 1982, 27; in addition, the Juvenile Court judge is allowed considerable discretion, see BGH NStZ 1986, 549 et seq.

12. see 7 below.

13. see <u>Pfeiffer</u> 1988, 96 et seq.

14. see <u>Dünkel</u> 1990, 89 et seq.; the Saarland is an exception, with a high proportion of young adults convicted according to juvenile criminal law (1989: 93%, see Figure 1).

15. see <u>Eisenberg</u> 1991, marginal note 3 referring to paragraph 105, with further references.

16. see <u>Cornils</u> 1985, 503 et seq.

17.   see <u>Cornils</u> 1985, 504.

18.   see <u>Cornils</u> 1988, 1295 et seq.

19.   see <u>Home Office</u> (Ed): "Prison Statistics England and Wales 1989", London 1990, 64; At 30 June 1985 there were 8 676 convicted offenders in juvenile establishments, but only 7 076 (= -18%) in 1989. In adult prisons, average occupation for the same period rose from 26 412 to 30 660 (= +16%, see page 18).

20.   Accordingly, the average length of sentence for 14-16 year old males fell from 4,9 months in 1982 to 3,4 months in 1985, but then rose again until 1989 to 4,4 months (with a substantial decline in absolute figures, partly as a result of cases being dropped and other measures) see <u>Home Office</u> (ed): "Criminal Statistics England and Wales 1988. London 1989", 140; 1989. London 1990, 170; among 17-20 year olds the average length of custodial sentences (generally falling) tended to increase (from 8,5 to 11,1 months), although among over-20 year olds an even more marked trend towards longer sentences could be observed in the course of the 1980s (see <u>Dünkel</u> 1990, 534). The lengthening of average prison sentences accordingly reflects (at least in the 1980s) no increased severity in sentencing, but is due to a reduction in short sentences in favour of non-custodial measures.

21.   see <u>Home Office</u> (ed): op. cit (Note 20), 168 et seq.

22.   see <u>Tutt</u> 1986a.

23.   see <u>Tutt/Giller</u> 1987.

24.   see, summarising, <u>Dünkel</u> 1990, 534 et seq.

25.   See above note 21.

26.   see <u>Home Office</u> 1990, 43 et seq.

27.   see <u>Home Office</u> 1990, 45; however, section 53 of the Children and Young Persons Act 1933 provides for prison sentences up to the maximum for adults to be inflicted also on under-18 year-olds for murder and manslaughter. The same applies to offences punishable with sentences of at least 14 years (for example, rape, robbery, burglary).

28.   see, summarising, <u>Jung</u> 1985, 713 et seq.

29.   see <u>Gordon</u> 1981, 64 et seq.; <u>Renton/Brown</u> 1987, 402 et seq.

30.   see <u>Picotti and de Strobel</u> 1986, 920.

31.   see <u>Beristain/Martin</u> 1986, 866 et seq.

32.   see Isphording/Spaniol 1985, 760 et seq.

33.   see Ministère de la Justice 1990 clauses 50 and 55 of the bill and explanatory report, 22 *et seq.*; see also Dünkel 1990a, 11 *et seq.*

34.   see Chaidou 1986, 1001 et seq.

35.   see Trechsel 1989, marginal note 26 referring to article 64.

36.   According to a judgment of the Austrian Supreme Court (Volume 40, No 3) special leniency is also applicable where the age limit of 21 is slightly exceeded, see Foregger/Serini 1988, II. with reference to article 34; irrespective of this age limit, article 34.1 of the Criminal Code provides for leniency where educational shortcomings are directly relevant to the offence.

37.   See overview in Dünkel 1990, 531 et seq.

38.   see chapter 26, para 4 (1) and (2) Swedish Criminal Code; Cornils 1985, 501 et seq.

39.   see Cornils 1985, 502 for the year 1982.

40.   see Lahti 1985, 429.

41.   see Pellinen 1991, 14 ff.

42.   This is illustrated by German juvenile criminal law: where young adults are not covered by juvenile criminal law under Section 105 JGG (see 3 above), the court can impose a prison sentence of 10-15 years instead of life imprisonment. A sentence to preventive detention is prohibited (see Section 106 (1) and (2) JGG).

43.   According to Feld 1987, 505 et seq, this is true of 11 states of the USA.

44.   see H-J Albrecht 1986, 1218 et seq., 1298.

45.   see Huber 1985, 681.

46.   see Dupont/Walgrave 1985, 540.

47.   see Scholten/ten Siethoff 1985, 574.

48.   see Bundesministerium der Justiz 1989; 1989a; Heinz 1990.

49.   see Heinz 1990, 213 et seq.; 1991.

50.   see in this respect Heinz 1987.

51.   The courts had partly recognised the admissibility of community service as an educative measure if related to educational shortcomings in connection with the attitude to work, see for example BGH in Holtz MDR 1976, 634; Bayerisches Oberlandesgericht Strafverteidiger 1984, 254; OLG Karlsruhe, Die Justiz 1988, 488 et seq. There was accordingly a need to make work orders possible as disciplinary measures, if it needed to be firmly brought home to the juvenile that he must take the consequences of his wrong-doing (Section 13 sub-section 1 JGG; see - also in relation to replacement of payment orders in the case of offenders without means and efforts to replace juvenile detention - Bundestags-Drucksache 11/5829, 18).

52.   see in this respect Busch/Hartmann/Mehlich 1986.

53.   On experiments with corresponding pilot schemes, see Dünkel/Mérigeau 1990, 95 et seq.; an insight into the progress of mediation projects in Germany is given by Schreckling, 1991; for the situation on mediation projects in England and Wales, see Marshall/Merry 1990.

54.   see, for an overview, Dünkel 1990, 96, 461.

55.   In absolute terms, the decrease was 3,529 (from 7,239 on 31.3.1983 to 3,710 on 30.9.1990 = -49%). The decrease to be expected for demographic reasons was approximately 20%, see also Dünkel 1987, 18 et seq.; 1990, 154 et seq.

56.   see Dünkel 1990, 173 et seq.

57.   On work education institutions, see in detail Rehberg 1989, 84 et seq.

58.   see Baechtold 1990, 63.

59.   Of the 18,860 18-25 year-olds convicted in 1987 only 58 (= 0.3%) were referred to a work education institution, according to the calculations of the Bundesamt für Statistik (ed.): Strafurteile 1987, Bern 1988.

60.   see Baechtold 1990, 74.

61.   see for recidivism statistics in Switzerland Besozzi 1989, 115 et seq.

62.   see Lopes Rocha 1986, 892.

63.   see Sections 6 and 10 of Act No. 401/82 of 23.9.1982 (German translation in Lopes Rocha 1986, 902 et seq.).

64.   see Section 4 of Act No. 401/82 in conjunction with Articles 73 and 74 of the Portuguese Criminal Code.

65.   For educational reasons young adults can remain in juvenile detention centres up to the age of 24, see Lopes Rocha 1986, 900.

66.   see Statistisches Bundesamt Wiesbaden (ed): Rechtspflege Reihe 3. Strafverfolgung 1989. Wiesbaden 1990, 60; regarding corresponding practice in previous years see Dünkel 1990, 94 et seq.

67.   see Home Office (ed.): Criminal Statistics in England and Wales 1989. London 1990, 163 et seq.; for girls the discontinuation figures are comparable but higher: 10-14 year-olds: 64%; 14-17 year olds: 51% and 17-20 year olds 33% (1989).

68.   see Scholten/ten Siethoff 1985, 592; Junger-Tas/Kruissink 1990, 29 et seq.; see regarding discontinuation practice also Sagel-Grande 1985, 216 et seq.

69.   see Junger-Tas/Kruissink 1990, 31.

70.   see Klages 1985, 394 et seq.; Lahti 1985, 456; in detail, Dünkel 1991.

71.   see Cornils 1985, 513 (1980: 17%); to this extent there seems to be hardly any difference in relation to older adults, with 14% discontinuations among 21-25 year-olds.

72.   An exception since 1974 had been the warning under Section 12, sub-section 1, Austrian JGG in cases where it was to be expected that the court would pronounce a discharge on grounds of "insufficient gravity of the offence" (Article 42, Austrian Criminal Code); however, this method was used until the early 1980s in only about 11% of convictions, see Dearing 1985, 264, 272. Discontinuation of proceedings by the prosecution only became significant (at regional level) in connection with conflict resolution pilot projects. For instance, in Linz the proportion of discontinuations of proceedings increased from 68% to 83% over the period 1984-1986, whereas in Salzburg and Vienna juvenile **court** decisions predominate, see Pelikan/Pilgram 1988, 70 et seq., 197.

73.   see Bogensberger 1991, 237 et seq.; as was to be expected, the proportion of discontinuations was higher (82.1%) in the district courts, which have jurisdiction for minor offences; a problem is raised however by the still very varied practice as between the regions, implying differences in the degree of acceptance by judges and prosecutors, with a more liberal approach in the western court districts, see page 238 et seq.

74.   In 1973 the conviction rate was as high as 55%, see Bogensberger 1991, 240.

75.   see Heinz/Hügel 1987, 43 et seq.; in general, offender-specific characteristics clearly play no more than a marginal role in comparison with a criminal record (and offence-related characteristics such as the extent of damage).

76.   see Home Office 1988, 5 et seq.

77.   see Home Office 1988, 6.

78.   see Home Office 1990, 43 et seq.

79.   see Dünkel 1990, *25 et seq*

80.   see Dünkel 1990, 127.

81.   see Pfeiffer 1988, 127; see also Pfeiffer 1991, 121.

82.   see Pfeiffer 1991, 114 et seq.

83.   see Dünkel 1990, 128.

84.   see Heinz 1990a; Pfeiffer 1991, 125 et seq., with further references.

85.   see BGHSt 11, 169 et seq.

86.   see Dünkel 1990, 466 with further references.

87.   see Bundestagsdrucksache 11/4892 of 26.6.1989.

88.   see for example Resolution No. 10, No.2e adopted at the 8th United Nations Congress on the Prevention of Crime and Treatment of Offenders in Havana in 1990 (United Nations doc A/Conf.144/28, 164 et seq.); for an international comparison of detention pending trial see Dünkel/Vagg 1992.

89.   see Dünkel 1990, 372; the ratios remain constant (per 100,000 in the age-group) despite the remarkable drop in figures of more than 50% since the mid-1970s.

90.   see Dünkel 1990, 375.

91.   see, in detail, Dünkel 1990, 373 et seq.; these are mainly forms of crisis intervention, shock treatment through detention and other preventive measures, which have nothing to do with detention on grounds related to the safeguarding of proceedings.

92.   On pilot projects in Germany, see Dünkel 1990, 390 et seq.

93.   see Dünkel/Vagg 1992.

94.   Of prisoners not yet finally convicted on 17.3.1988, 17% had begun their sentence early, see Schweizerisches Bundesamt für Statistik (ed.): Kriminalstatistik Nr. 7. Die Untersuchungshaft. Bern 1988, 1.

95.   see on the controversy, Eisenberg 1991, marginal note 18 referring to paragraph 93; Dünkel 1990, 365.

96.   see Dünkel 1990, 370.

97.   see Ministère de la Justice 1990, Materialien, 107.

98.   see <u>Ministère de la Justice</u> 1990, Clause 23 of the Bill. For offences punishable with up to seven years' imprisonment detention pending trial may not exceed one month, with a single possible extension of one month in exceptional cases. In all other cases an absolute maximum of one year applies.

99.   see <u>Home Office</u> (ed.): Prison Statistics England and Wales 1989. London 1990, 10, 39 et seq.

100.   see <u>Beristain/Martin</u> 1986, 879 et seq.

101.   see <u>Beristain/Martin</u> 1986, 880.

102.   see <u>Dünkel</u> 1990, 173 et seq.

103.   see regarding Sweden, <u>Bishop</u> 1991.

104.   see regarding the Ringe Institution <u>Driebold/Katoh</u> 1983.

105.   see <u>Dünkel</u> 1990, 468 et seq.

106.   see, with reference to the Austrian JGG of 1989 <u>Held/Jesionek</u> 1989; summarising, <u>Dünkel</u> 1990, 527 et seq.

Bibliography

Albrecht, H-J: "Entwicklungstendenzen des Jugendkriminalrechts und stationärer Freiheitsentziehung bei jugendlichen Straftätern in den USA". In: Dünkel, F; Meyer, K (Hrsg): *Jugendstrafe und Jugendstrafvollzug.* Teilband 2, Freiburg 1986, S.1211-1305.

Asbrock, B: "Plädoyer für ein Jungtäterrecht". *ZRP* 10 (1977), S.191-195.

Baechtold, A: *Straf- und Maßnahmenvollzug.* Bern 1990.

Beristain, A; Martin, J: "Jugendkriminalität und ihre Sanktionierung in Spanien". In: Dünkel, F; Meyer, K (Hrsg): *Jugendstrafe und Jugendstrafvollzug.* Teilband 2, Freiburg 1986, S.849-890.

Besozzi, C: "Rückfall nach Strafvollzug. Eine empirische Untersuchung". In: Kunz, K-L (Hrsg): *Die Zukunft der Freiheitsstrafe.* Bern 1989, S.115-141.

Bishop, N: Sweden. In: van Zyl Smit, D; Dünkel, F (Hrsg): *Imprisonment Today and Tomorrow - International Perspectives on Prisoners' Rights and Prison Conditions.* Deventer 1991, S.599-631.

Bogensberger, W: "Strafrecht (fast) ohne Strafe: Das neue österreichische Jugendgerichtsgesetz". *DVJJ-Journal* 2 (1991), S.235-242.

Bundesministerium der Justiz (Hrsg): *Jugendstrafrechtsreform durch die Praxis.* Bonn 1989.

Bundesministerium der Justiz (Hrsg): *"Diversion" im deutschen Jugendstrafrecht.* Bonn 1989a.

Busch, M; Hartmann, G; Mehlich, N: *Soziale Trainingskurse im Rahmen des Jugendgerichtsgesetzes.* 3. Aufl. Bonn (Bundesministerium der Justiz) 1986.

Chaidou, A: "Freiheitsentziehende Maßnahmen gegenüber jugendlichen Delinquenten in Griechenland". In: Dünkel, F; Meyer, K (Hrsg): *Jugendstrafe und Jugendstrafvollzug.* Teilband 2, Freiburg 1986, S.997-1049.

Cornils, K: "Freiheitsstrafe und Strafvollzug bei Jugendlichen in Schweden". In: Dünkel, F; Meyer, K (Hrsg): *Jugendstrafe und Jugendstrafvollzug.* Teilband 1, Freiburg 1985, S.497-534.

Cornils, K: "Schweden". In: Eser, A; Huber, B (Hrsg): *Strafrechtsentwicklung in Europa* 2. Teil 2, Freiburg 1988, S.1287-1345.

Dearing, A: "Freiheitsstrafe und Strafvollzug bei Jugendlichen in Österreich". In: Dünkel, F; Meyer, K (Hrsg): *Jugendstrafe und Jugendstrafvollzug.* Teilband 1, Freiburg 1985, S.259-316.

Driebold, R; Katoh, H: "Das Staatsgefängnis Ringe - Tendenzen des Strafvollzugs in Dänemark". In: Driebold, R (Hrsg): *Strafvollzug. Erfahrungen, Modelle, Alternativen.* Göttingen 1983, S.144-159.

Dünkel, F: *Die Herausforderung der geburtenschwachen Jahrgänge. Aspekte der Kosten-Nutzen-Analyse in der Kriminalpolitik.* Freiburg 1987.

Dünkel, F: "La privation de liberté à l'égard des jeunes délinquants. Tendances actuelles dans le cadre d'une comparaison internationale". In: Sace, J; van der Vorst, P (Hrsg): *Justice et jeunes délinquants.* Brüssel 1989, S.127-146.

Dünkel, F: *Freiheitsentzug für junge Rechtsbrecher. Zur Situation und Reform von Jugendstrafe, Jugendstrafvollzug, Jugendarrest und Untersuchungshaft in der Bundesrepublik Deutschland und im internationalen Vergleich.* Bonn 1990.

Dünkel, F: "Frankreich: Richtiger Schritt. Der Gesetzentwurf zur Reform des Jugendstrafrechts in Frankreich". *Neue Kriminalpolitik* 2 (1990a), Heft 4, S.11-12.

Dünkel, F: "Das deutsche Jugendgerichtsgesetz im europäischen Vergleich": In: Walter, M (Hrsg): *Probleme des Jugendkriminalrechts.* 2. Kölner Symposium. Bonn (Bundesministerium der Justiz) 1991, im Druck.

Dünkel, F; Mérigeau, M: "Les expériences de médiation délinquant-victime en République fédérale d'Allemagne". In: Dünkel, F; Zermatten, J (Hrsg): *Nouvelles Tendances dans le Droit Pénal des Mineurs.* Freiburg 1990, S.95-124.

Dünkel, F; Vagg, J: *Waiting for trial - International perspectives on the use of pre-trial detention and the rights and living conditions of prisoners waiting for trial.* Freiburg 1992, under preparation.

Dupont, L; Walgrave, L: "Jugendschutzgesetz und stationäre Unterbringung delinquenter Jugendlicher in Belgien". In: Dünkel, F; Meyer, K (Hrsg): *Jugendstrafe und Jugendstrafvollzug.* Teilband 1, Freiburg 1985, S.537-563.

Eisenberg, U: *Jugendgerichtsgesetz mit Erläuterungen.* 4. Aufl, München 1991.

Feld, B C: "The Juvenile Court meets the Principle of the Offence: Legislative Changes in Juvenile Waiver Statutes". *Journal of Criminal Law and Criminology 78* (1987), S.471-533.

Foregger, E; Serini, E: "Strafgesetzbuch". *Kurzkommentar.* 4. Aufl. Wien 1988.

Gordon, G H: *The Criminal Justice (Scotland) Act 1980.* Edinburgh 1981.

Heinz, W: "Neue ambulante Maßnahmen nach dem Jugendgerichtsgesetz". *MschrKrim* *70* (1987), S.129-154.

Heinz, W: "Die Jugendstrafrechtspflege im Spiegel der Rechtspflegestatisken. Ausgewählte Daten für den Zeitraum 1955-1988". *MschrKrim 73* (1990), S.210-227.

Heinz, W; Hügel, C: *Erzieherische Maßnahmen im deutschen Jugendstrafrecht.* 3. Aufl. Bonn (Bundesministerium der Justiz) 1987.

Home Office (Hrsg): *Punishment, Custody and the Community.* London 1988.

Home Office (Hrsg): *Crime, Justice and Protecting the Public. The Government's Proposals for Legislation.* London 1990.

Huber, B: "Jugendstrafe und Jugendstrafvollzug im Umbruch - Stationäre Maßnahmen in der Jugendkriminalrechtspflege in England und Wales". In: Dünkel, F; Meyer, K (Hrsg): *Jugendstrafe und Jugendstrafvollzug.* Teilband 1, Freiburg 1985, S.669-754.

Isphording, A; Spaniol, M: "Jugendstrafe und Jugendstrafvollzug in Frankreich". In: Dünkel, F; Meyer, K (Hrsg) : *Jugendstrafe und Jugendstrafvollzug.* Teilband 1, Freiburg 1985, S.755-844.

Jesionek, U; Held, K: *Jugendgerichtsgesetz 1988.* Wien 1989.

Jung, H: "Das schottische Children's Hearing System". In: Herzberg, R D (Hrsg): *Festschrift für D Oehler.* Köln u a 1985, S.705-727.

Junger-Tas, J; Kruissink, M: *Ontwikkeling van de jeugdcriminaliteit: periode 1980-1988.* Arnhem (WODC) 1990.

Kaiser, G: *Gesellschaft, Jugend und Recht.* Weinheim, Basel 1977.

Kaiser, G: "International vergleichende Perspektiven zum Jugendstrafrecht". In: Schwind, H-D u a (Hrsg): *Festschrift für G Blau.* Berlin, New York 1985, S.441-457.

Klages, J: "Freiheitsstrafe und Strafvollzug für Jugendliche in Dänemark". In: Dünkel, F; Meyer, K (Hrsg): *Jugendstrafe und Jugendstrafvollzug.* Teilband 1, Freiburg 1985, S.391-423.

Lahti, R: "Freiheitsstrafe und Jugendgefängnis in Finnland". In: Dünkel, F; Meyer, K (Hrsg): *Jugendstrafe und Jugendstrafvollzug.* Teilband 1, Freiburg 1985, S.425-461.

Lopes Rocha, M A: "Die Reform des Jugendstrafrechts in Portugal". In: Dünkel, F; Meyer, K (Hrsg): *Jugendstrafe und Jugendstrafvollzug.* Teilband 2, Freiburg 1986, S.891-903.

Marshall, T F, Merry, S: *Crime and Accountability: Victim/Offender Mediation in Practice.* London (HMSO) 1990.

Mechler, A: "Forensische Psychiatrie". In: Kaiser, G u a (Hrsg): *Kleines Kriminologisches Wörterburch.* 2. Aufl. Heidelberg 1985, S.106-110.

Ministère de la Justice (Hrsg): *Réponses à la Délinquance des Mineurs.* Paris 1990.

Pelikan, C; Pilgram, A: "Die "Erfolgsstatistik" des Modellversuchs". *Kriminalsoziologische Bibliographie 15* (1988), Heft 58/59, S.55-110.

Pellinen, T: "Finnland. Sanktionensystem im Umbruch". *Neue Kriminalpolitik 3* (1991), Heft 1, S.14-15.

Pfeiffer, C: *Jugendkriminalität und jugendstrafrechtliche Praxis - eine vergleichende Analyse zu Entwicklungstendenzen und regionalen Unterschieden.* Hannover (Expertise zum 8. Jugendbericht) 1988.

Pfeiffer, C: "Unser Jugendstrafrecht - Eine Strafe für die Jugend"? *DVJJ-Journal 2* (1991), S.114-129.

Picotti, L; de Strobel, G: "Freiheitsentziehende Maßnahmen gegenüber Minderjährigen und Jugendstrafvollzug in Italien". In: Dünkel, F; Meyer, K (Hrsg): *Jugendstrafe und Jugendstrafvollzug.* Teilband 2, Freiburg 1986, S.905-996.

Pieplow, L: "Erziehung als Chiffre". In: Walter, M (Hrsg): *Beiträge zur Erziehung im Jugendkriminalrecht.* Köln u a 1989, S.5-57.

Rehberg, J: "Grundriß Strafrecht II. Strafen und Maßnahmen". *Jugendstrafrecht.* 5. Aufl. Zürich 1989.

Renton, R W; Brown, H H: *Criminal procedure according to the law of Scotland.* Edinburgh 1983 et seq.

Sagel-Grande, J: "Die in den Niederlanden nicht zur richterlichen Aburteilung gelangende Kriminalität und ihr Umfang". *MschrKrim 68* (1985), S.216-228.

Scholten, H-J; ten Siethoff, F G A: "Jugendstrafe und Jugendstrafvollzug in den Niederlanden". In: Dünkel, F; Meyer, K (Hrsg): *Jugendstrafe und Jugendstrafvollzug.* Teilband 1, Freiburg 1985, S.565-666.

Schreckling, J: *Bestandsaufnahme zur Praxis des Täter-Opfer-Ausgleichs in der Bundesrepublik Deutschland.* Bonn (Bundesministerium der Justiz) 1991.

Trechsel, S: "Schweizerisches Strafgesetzbuch". *Kurzkommentar.* Zürich 1989.

Tutt, N: "Law and Policies on Juvenile Offending in England and Wales, Scotland, Northern Ireland and the Republic of Ireland". In: Kerner, H-J u a (Hrsg): *Jugendgerichtsbarkeit in Europa und Nordamerika - Aspekte und Tendenzen* - München 1986, S.469-502.

Tutt, N: *Managing a Diminishing Problem*. Manchester (Social Information Systems Ltd) 1986a.

Tutt, N; Giller, H: *The Elimination of Custody*. Unpublished MS, Lancaster 1987.

van Zyl Smit, D; Dünkel, F (Hrsg): *Imprisonment Today and Tomorrow. International Perspectives on Prisoners' Rights and Prison Conditions*. Deventer, Boston, 1991.

Figure 1

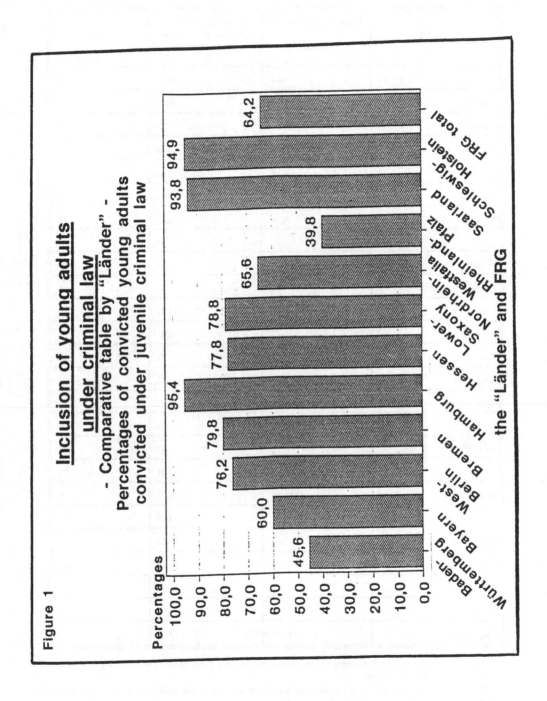

Figure 2: International comparison of the ages of criminal responsibility and majority (for criminal purposes and otherwise) in Europe

Country	Criminal responsibility (age)	Majority for criminal purposes (criminal law can/must apply) (age)	Majority (age)
Germany	14	18/21	18
UK/Wales	10/15*	18/21	18
Austria	14	19	19
Belgium	16**/18	16/18	18
Bulgaria	14	18	18
Denmark	15	15/18	18
Scotland	8/16	16/21	18
Spain	16	16	18
Finland	15	15/18	18
France	13	18	18
Greece	13	18/21	18
Netherlands	12	18/21	18
Hungary	14	18	18
Ireland	7/15***	18	18
Italy	14	18/21	18
Norway	15	18	18
Poland	13	18	18
Portugal	16	16/21	18
Romania	16/18	16/18/21	18
Sweden	15	15/18	18
Switzerland	7/15	15/18	20
Czechoslovakia	15	18	18
Turkey	11	15	18
Soviet Union	14****/16	14/16	18
Yugoslavia	14/16***	18/21	18

*	age at which a young offender may be detained in an institution for young offenders
**	traffic offences only
***	age at which a young offender may be detained in a prison institution for young offenders
****	particularly serious offences only

YOUNG ADULT OFFENDERS IN THE NEW EUROPEAN CONTEXT

REPORT

Mr K. Bard,
Deputy Secretary of State
Ministry of Justice (Hungary)

I. Preliminary remarks

There is probably a general expectation in the western world that the new questions arising out of the dramatic changes in the central and eastern European region and the pressure to react to them in the area of crime policy may give new impetus to criminological thinking in Europe as a whole. It is probably this expectation that made the planners of the colloquium decide to have a separate report prepared which is intended to comprise all aspects of young adult criminality from the angle of the former socialist countries.

It is, of course, a challenging task to give an overall picture on the basis of comparative research ranging from statistical data to novel forms of social control under the changing socio-political conditions.

However, the rapporteur faces immense difficulties when attempting to draw a general overview. First, there is the problem of collecting the necessary information. Apart from the deficiencies of collecting statistical data on criminality and sentencing - in countries where this data has even been published - legislators, policy makers and even criminologists, as compared to their colleagues in western Europe, have paid little attention to the specific problems of the age-group concerned.

Furthermore, policy makers, for quite understandable reasons, seem to concentrate on issues others than those related to the needs of a particular section of the population. The main objective, consuming almost all intellectual resources, is to set up institutions which guarantee respect for the rule of law. Therefore, there remains little room for more specific problems for the time being.

Finally, as some kind of reaction to the ideology and rhetorics in the past, numerous experts in the eastern European region are inclined to overestimate the theses of the classical school of penal law and reject therefore any institution or treatment tailored to the individual needs of a certain type of offender, at least as far as formal social control is concerned.

However, it is evident that the rejection of the idea of individualised justice in its present unrefined and uncompromising form is but the expression of a temporary attitude determined by specific political conditions. It is obvious that the political, economic and social changes, or more precisely their negative side-effects - rising unemployment and economic hardship, etc. - are likely to affect the generation of young adults more than other sections of the population. As a consequence, one may reasonably assume that aftercare or probation as well as the entire system of social support, which after almost totally collapsing are to be set up on the basis of new principles, will attempt to ease the problems of young adults. Furthermore, one may also hope that newly established professional groups, voluntary associations and non-governmental organisations providing support for offenders and inmates which had almost no role to play in the past, will exert some influence on the legislative process and make decision-makers pay regard to the particular needs of that specific age group.

As a closing remark we should eliminate a misconception which seems to be widespread in the western world according to which the countries of the central and eastern European region could be treated as a homogenous entity. Even if certain common elements of a totalitarian political establishment and its ciminal policy implications could be identified in all the countries of the region the impact of

historical traditions has not been eliminated over the last forty years. Therefore, assertions that would be valid for the whole region may be formulated on an extremely general level only.

With a view to the considerations and difficulties outlined, the report is by necessity fragmentary as it has to focus on the Hungarian situation and solutions. Assertions for the whole region shall be formulated only where they may go beyond vacant generalisations.

II.   Crime in the period of transformation

The political crisis of the socialist political establishment has also become evident in that it can no longer cope with the phenomenon of crime. The erosion of the formerly tight control, characteristic of the authoritarian regime, as well as the almost complete collapse of the normative system are indicated by the increasing rate of crime. While in the period between 1966 and 1975 one could count with the relatively unchanged number of registered crimes of 120 000 per year and an almost stabile clearance rate in the following ten years the same number came to 140 000. Thus the number of crimes per 10 000 inhabitants amounted to 115 in the period 1965-1975 on average while in the following decade it rose to 130. In this latter period, the fall in the effectiveness of clearing up offences was already evident - indicated among other things by the growing number of unidentified offenders.

The dramatic change, however, took place in the years after 1985 when the number of registered crimes grew by 100 000 within five years, accompanied by a four times increase in the number of unidentified offenders. The explosion of crime and the enormous decline in police effectiveness indicated that the competent agencies completely lost control over criminality. In 1990 twice as many crimes were registered as in 1985 and only every third offender could be identified.

It would take us too long to go into the analysis of why the competent agencies completely lost control over criminality. We confine ourselves to the assumption that the crime control agencies and the administration of justice have been eroded along with all the institutions of the system. Legislation and law enforcement reacted on the visible crisis in a confused way with inconsequent measures declaring permissivness at certain times and calling for unreasonable rigour at others. The disconcerted approach arising out of panic could not, of course, stop the process in which the values protected by criminal law have been subjected to a general challenge.

114

Since the elections of last spring no considerable change has taken place, however certain elements of a new criminal policy have become visible already.

Among the factors that may have significant impact on the crime issue at present we refer, first of all, to the fact that there is complete agreement in today's Hungary as to the respect for human rights and basic political feedoms. This, of course, sets a limit to criminalisation. Certain tensions and conflicts within society that used to be solved by criminal law in the past have to be overcome by other methods.

When interpreting the rising crime rates we should bear in mind that it is not always the number of crimes that indicates the seriousness of the crime problem in the most proper way. In Hungary, for instance, it was in the fifties when the number of convicted persons was the highest, however, in this period citizens feared not so much those who were supposed to have violated but rather those who had enforced criminal law.

The main difficulties which the new government faces have their roots in the previous five years as indicated above. Public security deteriorated in that period to the extent that fear of crime among the population became a problem of public concern. This is first of all due to the fact that the number of criminal offences against personal property affecting a large proportion of the population, such as breaking and entering or theft from cars is three times higher today it was five years ago, while the number of robberies has doubled. In the same period the number of the most serious, but less visible, crimes against the person (murder, homicide, assault, etc.) has remained unchanged and violent crimes against sexual integrity have even become less frequent.

III. Legislation in the former socialist countries

Surveying the existing provisions on the status of young adults in the penal codes of various countries, one may make the following somewhat rough classification:

a. In some penal codes there are no specific provisions on young adults, however, the rules on how to implement prison sentences seem to guarantee that their treatment is different from that of adults, meaning that the rules on the institutional treatment of juveniles are extended to the age group of young adults.

b. According to another relatively widely known provision, young age is a mitigating circumstance under the law, therefore courts are obliged to impose lighter sentences for young adults - also in the case of juveniles - than for adult persons. As a general rule more lenient treatment also means that certain types of sanctions used with adults may not be imposed on either juveniles or young adults.

c. As to a further model, courts have a general authorisation to apply under certain conditions the set of provisions prescribed for juveniles in the penal code. In some countries it is in the courts' discretionary power to make use of this possibility while in others it is mandatory to apply the rules on juveniles to young adults as well provided the preconditions set up by the law are present.

In the overwhelming majority of the former socialist countries the provisions on the status of young adults in the penal codes follow the provision outlined in paragraph *a*.

As a general rule the penal codes do not use the notion of young adults and there are but a few provisions indicating that young offenders who are above the age of juveniles should not necessarily be subjected to the same institutional treatment as adult persons. The Hungarian legislation may serve as a representative example. According to the penal code of 1978 some of the rules prescribed for juveniles - namely persons between 14 and 18 years of age - are also to be applied to young people over 18, provided that at the time of committing the criminal offence they were not older than 18. Thus, convicts are placed in a juvenile prison unless they have reached the age of 21 at the time of the court decision. Also the term of the young persons stay in a juvenile reformatory may be extended until they have reached the age of 19 and can even last until the end of the school term in the same year. Mention should be made of two further provisions, which, however, due to legislative changes have no practical significance in Hungary anymore. Both the death penalty and the preventive detention of multiple recidivists could only be imposed on persons who at the time of the perpetration had already reached the age of 20. Preventive detention was abolished by parliament in 1989 while capital punishment was declared to be unconstitutional by the Constitutional Court and removed from the sanction system last year. While substantive penal law includes at least a few specific provisions which take into consideration that young adults may require different treatment from that of adults, the law on criminal procedure is completely indifferent to the problems of the age group concerned. The less formal procedure, tailored to the moral needs and the intellectual level of young persons, and designed to provide the courts with procedural tools so that they could find the proper individualised sanction may be used strictly in cases of juveniles. The moment the young person has reached his/her 18th year the rules of the general procedure have to be applied.

Similar to legislation, court practice does not attach much significance to the social and psychological characteristics of young adults either. According to the Supreme Court's guiding principle on sentencing the fact that the defendant is to be considered a young adult (as to the court practice this category comprises young people between 18 and 24) should be regarded as a factor mitigating the sentence. However, considering that in the same guiding principle the Supreme Court takes the stand that the offender's clean record is a mitigating circumstance as well with the exception of juveniles and young adults, one may draw the conclusion that by declaring that young age should be evaluated as a mitigating condition, the Supreme Court simply wished to avoid that young adults were placed into a more disadvantegous position than adult persons. Experience indicates that the Supreme Court's instruction has practical significance primarily in cases where the offender is slightly over 18.

Among the penal laws of central eastern Europe it is only the Yugoslav penal code which includes separate and detailed provisions on the status and treatment of young adults. Apart from providing information on the present legislation we consider it expedient to give a brief outline of the previous legislation since the historical sketch may help legislators in other countries to avoid certain mistakes when drafting provisions for young adults. Until 1959 the term of young adults as a category of penal law did not exist in Yugoslav legislation either. Individuals under 14 were regarded as children, their acts falling outside the scope of criminal law. The age group of those between 14 and 18 was divided into two categories: younger minors (14-16) and older minors. Offenders over 18 were treated according to the general rules applying for adults.

It was in 1959 when the category of young adults was introduced in Yugoslav criminal law. According to the relevant provision the court in exceptional cases could apply the educational measures, called increased supervision by a legal guardian, and send the offender to a correctional institution instead of imposing some kind of punishment for adults under the age of 21, provided the offender's mental capacities corresponded to those of minors (persons under 18). For the sake of clarity we add that the category of young adults implied persons who at the time of committing the criminal offence had not reached 18 years of age and who at the time of the court's final decision were not over 21.

No doubt the introduction of the category of young adults and the authorisation of the courts by the legislator to use educational measures for persons belonging to this age group instead of imposing punishment on them was a reflection of a more humane attitude as well as the result of the scientific assumption that the legal status of individuals entering adulthood should not be completely equal to that of adult offenders.

There was general agreement that some measures known before with respect to minors should only be extended to young adults under certain conditions.

In spite of this recognition and contrary to the legislator's intention there were altogether 20 to 30 cases per year throughout the country where courts made use of the new provision, while it is estimated that the number of defendants who could have benefited from the provisions in question amounted to between 8 000 and 10 000.

According to expert opinions the extremely rare application originated primarily in the deficiencies of the relevant legal provisions. Firstly, the wording of the law according to which educational measures could be applied in exceptional cases could only have made courts reluctant to make use of the possibility offered by the law. It was also argued that the number of educational measures to be used for young adults was far too low. But the main deficiency of the law that might explain the fiasco of the legislator's endeavour to provide for the specific treatment of young adults was that the use of the educational measures was made dependent upon the condition that the young adult's mental capacity corresponded to that of a person qualifying as a minor. Psychologists and psychiatrists pointed out that it was almost hopeless to determine a certain general level of the mental development of minors to which the mental capacity of a young adult could have been compared.

In addition to legislative deficiencies the lack of proper infrastructure might also have contributed to the courts' reluctance to use the relevant provisions. With the exception of larger cities the proper services which in theory could have carried out the medical psychological personality tests were missing.

Under these circumstances it is hardly surprising that judges were inclined to abstain from imposing educational measures on young adults. Recognising the weak points of the legal regulation legislators made considerable changes in 1976. Article 82 of the present criminal code of the SFRY provides that the court may pronounce a corresponding measure of increased supervision or an institutionalised educational measure in respect of perpetrators who qualify as young adults with a view to the personality of the defendant and the conditions under which the criminal offence was committed.

It follows from the regulation that the application of educational measures is not made dependent upon any particular condition; in principle they may be imposed on any young adult offender and for any criminal offence. The gravity of the offence committed as well as potential previous convictions have of course a considerable impact on the court's option.

In contrast to the law of 1959 the educational measures that may be pronounced by the court indicate a broad variety. Increased supervision may be pronounced to be exercised by parents or guardians, or by some other family or guardianship bodies. As far as institutional educational measures are concerned the court has an option to send the young adult offender to an educational or a correctional institution or to order him to be placed in a treatment institution.

Educational measures ordered by the court may last until the person reaches 23 years of age.

On the basis of the rather flexible provisions of the Yugoslav penal code one could reasonably expect that courts make use of imposing educational measures to a broader extent. However statistical data prove the opposite: courts continued to give preference to suspended imprisonment and other "traditional" penal sanctions used for adults and imposing educational measures remained restricted to exceptional cases. In the period between 1985 and 1989 there were 199 cases altogether in the whole country where courts decided to give priority to educational measures. Thus Yugoslav court practice seems to refuse the criminological category of young adults in spite of the legislator's decision to provide for particular treatment of this age group.

From among the legislations of the former socialist countries the Polish provision deserves mention as well. According to Article 9 of the Polish penal code of 1969 individuals over 17 shall be liable under criminal law, that is, persons under 17 are dealt with on the basis of a special legislation of 1982 on the administration of justice in the case of juveniles.

The age limit set down in the penal code is, however, flexible. On the one hand, in cases of serious crimes against life, serious rape, robbery and some other offences laid down in the law, the alleged offender may be subject to criminal liability after attaining the age of 16. On the other hand, with regard to perpetrators committing less serious offences the court may order educational or corrective measures prescribed for juveniles instead of imposing punishment.

Particular provisions apply for persons who may come under the category of young adults, namely individuals who at the time of the court decision have not attained their 21 year of age (Article 120, paragraph 4). The provision on sentencing calls on the court to pay due regard to the educational impact the sanction may exert on the offender (Article 51). As far as the detailed rules are concerned several provisions prove the legislator's intention to have persons under 21 treated in a more lenient way as compared to the general rule. Thus the provision on extraordinary mitigation may be used "in especially justified cases" for young people. Also, conditional release may be granted at an earlier stage if the person qualifies as a young adult. According to the general rule convicts may be released after having served two thirds of their sentence while in the case of persons under 21 release can already be granted after having served half of the term.

In contrast to the provisions enlisted above providing for a more lenient treatment of young adults the section on conditional release reflects a different attitude. While in ordinary cases imprisonment may be suspended for a period 2 to 5 years the minimum probation term for young adults is 3 years.

Mention should be made of the draft for a new penal code for Poland since the drafters plan to extend the category of young adults. In the present law the particular provisions mentioned above concern persons who at the time of the court's decision did not reach 21 years of age. Article 113, paragraph 7 of the draft provides that the rules on sentencing, conditional release, conditional imprisonment (outlined above) should apply to persons who at the time of the perpetration have not attained 21 years of age unless they are over 24 at the time of the first instance court decision.

IV. Criminality of young adults

In this section we will attempt to give an overview on the sentencing practice of Hungarian courts. The data on young adult cases, however, say little unless we provide proper measures of comparison. Therefore, we will give the data on the sentencing practice of Hungarian courts on young adults, referring also, however, to two further age groups: to juveniles (14-18 years of age) and to adults (according to the legal definition of all persons over 18).

In order to threw some light on at least one possible factor that may explain potential differences in the sentencing pattern, we will make a brief comparison of the dissimilarities in the registered criminal behaviour of the three age groups concerned.

Individuals belonging to all three age groups are sentenced most frequently for property crimes: in the case of young adults, sentences for property crimes represent around 50 per cent of all court sentences, the corresponding ratios in case of juveniles and adults being 70 and 40 per cent respectively.

Traffic offences are second in rank order in the case of both young adults and adult persons, but are fourth in rank order in the case of juveniles.

The next goup of offences are those against public order as far as young adults are concerned. Public order offences comprising a broad variety of illegal conduct, ranging from crimes against public safety like terrorist acts or abuse of firearms and public order in the narrower sense including incitement against minorities, against legal provisions or hooliganism to crimes against public health such as environmental offences and drug offences, take fourth place in the case of adults and second as far as juveniles are concerned.

The next category for young adults is crimes against the person (the most serious being murder, homicide and assault) figuring in third place in the case of juveniles and adults and fourth place as far as young adults are concerned. In order to avoid misunderstandings it should be stressed that we are following the structure and the provisions of the present Hungarian penal code: the chapter on crimes against the person mentions only some violent crimes.

Based on the analysis of the Hungarian data we may make certain further observations which are likely to be valid for the other countries of the region as well. Thus, the criminal behaviour of those between 18 and 20 indicates numerous similarities with that of the age group under 18 while the criminal behaviour of those between 20 and 24 clearly shows the traits of this transitional period in the individual's life.

A further general observation may be that young adults represent a rather active section of the population as far as criminal conduct is concerned. The following table shows the proportion of the various age groups among registered offenders as a whole in 1990.

Age group	1990 %	1989 %
Juveniles (14-17)	11.5	11.2
Young adults (18-24)	25.1	22.7
25-39	42.6	44.2
40-49	14.0	14.3
50-59	5.0	5.5
Over 60	1.8	2.1

Regarding the dynamics of the young adults' share among all registered offenders a slight increase may be perceived: in 1987 there were 19,455 young adult offenders registered who made up 21 per cent of all registered offenders; the relevant figures for

1988 are 17,211 and 20,9 per cent respectively. As indicated by the above table the ratio of young adults and juveniles among all registred offenders has increased in the last two years as well.

Concerning the number of convicted persons and their ratio among all individuals convicted by the courts the same trend may be observed. In 1987 the 15,069 young adults made up 22,5 per cent of all convicted persons, the relevant data for 1988 and 1989 being 15,274 (23,1 per cent) and 14,934 (23,8 per cent). A further increase is proven by the statistical data from 1990 according to which young adult offenders represent 26,7 per cent of all individuals convicted by the courts - 12,427. The decrease in the absolute number of convicted persons concerning all age groups is mostly due to the acts on amnesty enacted in 1990.

Considering the fact that young adults (together with juveniles) are overrepresented among offenders of property crimes where the clearance rate is extremely low we may reasonably assume that their criminal activity has increased more intensively than indicated by the police and court statistics. (Because of the more sophisticated and organised way of perpetration the clearance rate in case of young adults is probably lower than where juveniles are the offenders.)

A further characteristic trait of the criminality of young adults in Hungary is their relatively high proportion among offenders of robbery, rape and some other violent crimes. In this connection it is worth mentioning that in the course of the preparations to the present penal code (dating back to 1978) it was considered introducing specific provisions and sanctions for young adults.

The research initiated by the drafting committee indicated that the particular social status, intellectual and emotional level of young adults may require treatment similar to that of juveniles. Therefore the research team came up with the proposal to introduce a model similar to that adopted by the Yugoslav code.

The drafting committee, however, refused to accept the recommendation arguing that criminal activity of young adults was extremely intensive particularly within the realm of violent crimes. It was feared that the extension of the milder treatment of juveniles to young adults may run counter to the needs of effective crime control.

V. Sentencing practice of the courts

It is partly the lack of special provisions in the Hungarian penal code which may explain that the sentencing practice of the courts in the case of adult offenders and young adults is rather similar. The most common type of sanction imposed on both categories is fines (in the adult cases 44 per cent, in the case of young adults 37 per cent in 1990). Conditional imprisonment was used in 26 per cent of all cases with young adults in 1990, the corresponding ratio in the case of adults came up to 24 per cent.

Penal measures - the most significant of them being penal warning in case of minor offences and probation -take third place for both young adults and adults (in

1990, 17 and 15 per cent respectively) followed by suspended imprisonment for both age groups.

The sentencing practice of the Hungarian courts in juvenile cases is somewhat different, primarily because of the special regulations in the penal code. The penal measure, called reformatory, can only be used for persons under 18 and probation may be imposed on juveniles to a broader extent than it is in the case of offenders over 18.

Therefore penal measures are applied in almost 60 per cent of all juvenile cases, followed by suspended imprisonment and unconditional prison. Fines play a less important role again because of the specific provisions in the penal code: the courts may impose fines on those offenders only if they have their own earnings.

Apart from the lack of specific provisions in the penal code as indicated above some further factors may also explain the similarity in the sentencing practice in young adult and adult cases.

The high ratio of unconditional imprisonment might be the consequence of the fact that while young age is considered as a mitigating circumstance, this is "counterbalanced" by the fact that young adults are overrepresented among the perpetrators of violent crimes.

Furthermore, it is important to note that the ratio of recidivists is almost equal in both categories: 30 per cent in the case of young adults and 36 as far as adult perpetrators are concerned. The proportion of multiple recidivists comes to 9 per cent among young adults, their proportion among adult offenders is 15 per cent.

The data on the sentencing practice of the courts in Poland are also available. In 1989 the number of convicts qualifying as young adults came to 14,359. Almost 30 per cent of them were sentenced to unconditional imprisonment, the most "popular" non custodial sanction being suspended imprisonment (48,7 per cent), while in 11,6 per cent of the cases fines were imposed. Unfortunately, the difference in both age groups concerned and the sanctions available for the courts make comparison between the Polish and the Hungarian sentencing practice almost impossible.

VI. Drug offences

In relation to the drug problem in central and eastern Europe we should first make ot clear that it was only in the early eighties that public discussion on the issue first began.

Therefore numerous crucial problems that have to be overcome in order to find the proper reaction to this type of deviance still exist.

As far as the history of drug abuse in Hungary is concerned we may distinguish four periods. From the mid- sixties to 1970 drug abuse was a sporadic phenomenon. (The first drug related death was reported in the year 1969 which was the same time that the first police reports on drug consuming groups were prepared.) It was in the seventies when Hungary started to get confronted with the drug problem. An increasing number of middle and lower-middle class young people abused drugs and medicine at parties, usually mixing it with alcohol. The limited scope of the problem was indicated, however, by the fact that drug abuse was almost exclusively restricted to the capital. The next step started in 1973 and lasted to the early eighties. This was the period when drug abuse began to spread all over the country, mainly in the form of "glue sniffing", which was frequently combined with the abuse of alcohol and medicine. The typical way of obtaining drugs was forging prescriptions but the number of burglaries in pharmacies increased as well. In the fourth stage, which began in the early eighties, abuse definitely spread. This fourth phase indicated at the same time a dramatic turn in the domain of the drug problem, perhaps in the whole region. While until the second half of the eighties it was the demand side exclusively, that is consumption and its consequences, that caused social and individual conflicts, the phenomena of the supply side (trafficking and related problems) are becoming evident nowadays. It should also be noted that there have been fundamental changes on the consumption side as well. Until recently consumption was restricted to various psychotropic substances, medicaments and sniffing organic solvents or glues. At present new abuse customs are beginning to spread among young people: such as drinking poppy-tea or the oral use of home made preparations of opium poppy straw or smoking cigarettes containing marihuana.

The number of reported crimes in Hungary has ranged from 130,000 to 150,000 per year in the eighties while there have been about 50,000 persons sentenced by the courts. In the same period the corresponding figures for drug offenders came to about 1,600 and 500 respectively, 90 per cent of them being sentenced for consumption.

75 per cent of the sentenced drug offenders belong to the age group of between 15 and 24, almost 42 per cent of them being young adults (between 18 and 24 years of age). Thus, it is evident that drug criminality is actually the criminality of the young generations. (It is remarkable that females, by their 20 per cent proportion, are overrepresented as compared to their general ratio among sentenced individuals.)

The sentences imposed on drug offenders reflect both the general characteristics of the age group concerned and the ambivalent attitude of the crime control agencies and courts to the drug problem.

The young offenders' poor financial conditions are reflected in the fact that fines for drug offences are imposed in a lower number of cases than the average. Suspended prison sentences, on the other hand, come to over 40 per cent, which is far higher than in the rest of the cases. The sentencing practice outlined indicates that proper sanctions for handling the drug problem are absent in the Hungarian penal system. The extension of forced medical treatment, originally destined to cure offenders with alcohol problems, to drug abusers turned out to be a fiasco and was never used in practice.

In almost every second case courts make use of the penal code's provision on extraordinary mitigation. This is clearly contrary to the legislator's intention, according to which this provision should be applied exclusively under exceptional circumstances, and in cases other than drug offences courts normally follow the legislator's instruction.

The sentencing practice of the courts is but one indication of a paradoxical situation in today's Hungary. On the one hand the drug problem is becoming more and more serious both in the demand and the supply area. The supply has increased considerably over the last two years by the opening of the frontiers. Various cannabis products and LSD are imported mainly from Turkey and the Netherlands to Hungary primarily by criminal organisations with the participation of Hungarian individuals living abroad. In the cities close to the frontier centres have been set up with the objective to distribute the products smuggled into the country. As a consequence of the events in Yugoslavia, Hungary is becoming one of the most significant transit roots for criminal organisations. As far as the demand side is concerned we have already referred to the recent spreading of new forms of consumption.

On the other hand the cases coming before the courts have dropped considerably together with the convictions (45 convictions in 1989 45 and 19 in 1990).

The lack of a consequent approach, the uncertainties as to the borderline between rational tolerance and permissivness emanating from weakness have led to the fact that the police have not really cared to clear up drug offences. Also, the far too lenient court sentences may have discouraged them to invest energy into prosecuting drug crimes. On the other hand the almost symbolic sanctions imposed by the courts may reflect the judges' growing awareness of the fact that the drug phenomenon should be at least partly treated by institutions falling outside the scope of criminal law.

The recent development in Hungarian legislation indicates a change in the policy of treating drug offenders. According to the bill on the amendment to the criminal code adopted by the government in October 1991 dealers and particularly those acting as members of criminal organisations should be punished by extremely severe sanctions. On the other hand persons who prepare, acquire or keep a small quantity of abusable drugs, for purposes other than putting them on market should have a chance to avoid criminal sanctions. In their cases the police should suspend procedure and if the individual proves to have undergone treatment for a certain time prosecution should be waived. This piece of legislation indicates the first step towards a more refined approach to the drug problem.

GENERAL REPORT

by
Mrs V. Lenoir-Degoumois,
General Rapporteur, Professeur Emeritus,
University of Lausanne (Switzerland)

INTRODUCTION

Towards the end of the nineteenth century and in the early years of the twentieth, a sweeping movement originating in the United States reached Europe; its aim was to remove minors from the scope of general criminal law and give them the benefit of a simultaneously protective and educational approach, taking more account of the young offender's personality and needs than of the offence committed. Specialised courts were set up to apply this new concept, and the juvenile court judge often became the main specialist in the protection of unfortunate children, until a host of offices and institutions were set up, especially after the second world war, to look after, protect, train and mend the ways of minors, whether they were offenders or not. To some extent, these have taken over from juvenile courts, and their social policies have stabilised, or even reduced, juvenile offences, with the help in some places of demographic trends.

This is why the problem of young adult offenders long went unnoticed in criminal and penological history. It has only been of interest to criminologists for the last twenty years or so. It is a well-known fact that, in our post-industrial societies - and especially in urban areas - there is a new phenomenon, a new age group between adolescence and adulthood, exhibiting specific psychological and social features and a criminal tendency which has certainly given rise to great concern. Contemporary criminologists, therefore, cannot fail to take an interest in these phenomena, and they are now trying to analyse this delinquency and work out a crime policy appropriate to these young adults.

1. WHO ARE YOUNG ADULTS ?

During the colloquium it has become apparent that their psychological and social characteristics make young adults as different from adolescents as from adults.

Research into developmental psychology has shown that young people go through intermediate stages of varying lengths and degrees of awkwardness before reaching adult maturity, characterised, for its part, by personal independence and an ability to find a place in society.

For centuries young people went through two conventional ritual transitions: from school to working life and from their original family to the family that they create. However the development of our post-industrial societies has partly done away with these landmarks, which used to make it easier for young people to integrate into society; rapid structural and/or cyclical changes are occurring in our European societies: in schooling, the labour market and family make-up. The extension of compulsory schooling is increasingly in demand, but would do nothing to prevent the failure at school of large numbers of disadvantaged pupils, the lowest levels of educational qualifications are being devalued, and the economic crisis is bringing unemployment and insecure jobs - especially to young people without skills or with low levels of training. All these factors delay young people's arrival in working life and the start of their careers. They are, as a result, relatively dependent financially and for accommodation on their original family and/or reliant on welfare benefits.

The current more liberal moral attitude to family matters makes it possible for them to put off starting their own family (within or outside wedlock) and forming a couple with a child for some time. Hence a good many young people escape the pressure to set up a stable, independent unit that was still felt a few decades ago.

In these circumstances, young adults in the age group 16/18 to 21/23 find it difficult to build up their psychological and social identity, floating in a limbo of latency and uncertainty in which their legitimate aspirations come up against harsh reality, which smashes their hopes and illusions and frustrates them to the point at which they despair and revolt, perhaps ending up by adopting deviant, or even delinquent conduct. Drug abuse is just one example of this existential malaise and this suffering.

2. YOUNG ADULT CRIMINALITY

The crime rate for adults and young adults alike has risen in the west since the end of the second world war, with a much sharper increase for the latter. There is consistency between official statistics and young adults' own accounts where the description of young adult criminality - namely in the 16/18 to 23 age group - in most western countries is concerned; this is the age group in which committing offences peaks, followed by a clear downward trend, and certainly from 25 onwards. So this criminality is usually of a temporary nature, a fact which should encourage society to show some patience in its reactions and in a desire to avoid over-stigmatising the offenders, most of whom are going through a transient phase.

It also has to be said that research ought subsequently to be done on the situation in eastern Europe, in order to ascertain how much of the crime there is committed by young adults. According to the information given to the colloquium, a soaring crime rate is currently being recorded there as a result of the political, economic and social changes and of fundamental shifts in values. Justice systems and infrastructure are experiencing a sea change, and police resources are often insufficient to identify offenders. In the circumstances, and at this stage, it seems too early to single out young adults.

Obviously this young adult crime does not include "white-collar" offences or serious economic crimes. It consists mainly of offences against property (such as theft, burglary, thefts of, and from, vehicles and deliberate damage). Most assaults and sexual offences are committed by an older age group. While the trend is upwards, the female crime rate is well below that of young men.

Great attention must be paid to the re-offending syndrome, as we know that the earlier a person is first convicted of an offence, the greater the risk of further offences.

Young adult crime is often associated with some degree of marginalisation, perhaps manifesting itself in risky, or even suicidal, behaviour, such as erratic driving, drug dependency, hooliganism at sports grounds or aggressiveness directed against minorities.

Criminological research has not yet ascertained whether their offences are more spontaneous than premeditated, but it certainly seems that the damage caused by this delinquency is frequently disproportionate to the acts committed.

To sum up, young adult crime is thus of a specific nature and type and has its own causes, re-offending pattern and development. It therefore requires appropriate reactions from society, whether in terms of prevention or of crime policy. Should we nevertheless make a distinction between those young adults without an official criminal record and those who have already offended ?

3.   CRIME POLICY IN RELATION TO YOUNG ADULTS

3.1   Prevention

"*If*", as the criminologist Marc Ancel wrote, "*certain kinds of antisocial or deviant behaviour and situations posing a risk to society can be explained, not by the dangerous nature of the individual concerned, but by his living conditions and social conditioning, it has to be accepted that punishment will be meaningful and really felt only if action is taken at the same time, or first, to improve these social conditions and this crime-generating environment. Reactions to crime thus involve action which is at least very largely part of general policy*". This statement is fully appropriate in relation to young adults.

It is therefore important, in every European country, to stress the preventive effort which is essential in relation to all young people, even where finance is scarce, if their legitimate need to find a place in society is to be satisfied. In any case, this is also an immediate consequence of the application of democratic values - to which present-day Europe aspires - based on respect for, and the human dignity of, every individual, and on greater social justice.

Those who addressed the colloquium were unanimous in stressing the need for educational preventive action starting in childhood, particularly in the shape of improved school and social services and the provision of facilities where the family environment is lacking. Self-evidently, the fight against drug abuse must play a prominent part in preventive efforts.

In spite of the economic crisis, states and private businesses must develop effective and motivating opportunities for work for young adults, replacing the short, successive training periods and insecure minor jobs which disadvantaged young adults trying to avoid unemployment too often find to be their only outlets.

In order to achieve this, should we reduce working hours in general and devise societies where workers agree to forego increased earnings and to divide their time between paid employment, voluntary community work and long periods of leisure, as recommended by certain social scientists who have immediately been termed Utopians?

This question has affected me personally, faced with the difficult problems of achieving the realistic and motivating integration of young adults !

For the purposes of prevention, the Colloquium rightly emphasised the need to develop technical means and deterrents as salutary ways of curbing the criminality of young adults who, at their age, are still likely to be receptive to these.

3.2 Crime policy proper

However, as well as the need to prevent offending by young adults and the essential development of appropriate social policy measures - about which there was unanimity - crime policy in respect of this age group was also the object of much attention, as it was the theme of the Colloquium. What are, in practice, the steps which society as a whole will take in response to young adult crime ?

Much emphasis was placed on the value of diversion measures, enabling young adults, even after committing an offence, to avoid being caught up in the criminal justice system. These are particularly welcome if they contain an element of reparation and are accompanied by sound back-up from skilled staff. However, in these circumstances, it is important not to underestimate the risks of a private justice regime, depriving young adults of the guarantees of their individual freedoms offered to them by court supervision and procedural rules.

In the face of the many problems which crime policy raises in respect of young adult offenders, this report, with a view to clarity, will single out the following themes and consider them in turn:

— the consistency of the legal system where the various ages of majority are concerned;
— the law applicable to young adult offenders;
— courts with jurisdiction in juvenile matters;
— the procedural rules to be applied;
— the basic principles of court reactions;
— the system of penalties.

Subsequent chapters will be devoted to the role of social and voluntary workers, the co-operation of those involved in crime policy and the arousing of public and media awareness; a final chapter will cover research.

3.2.1 Ages of majority

It was noted that there was no uniform legal model for the various European countries, which adopt a wide variety of approaches to matters of imputability and criminal responsibility.

Furthermore, the ages of civil and criminal majority are not always the same within one country; does the latter correspond only to the principle of criminal responsibility ?

And if there is a tendency to apply the same system to young adults as to juvenile delinquents, is there not a risk of a sort of "criminal minorisation", whereas they are regarded as responsible in the civil sphere ?

3.2.2 The law applicable to young adult offenders

This theme was one of the main points of the Colloquium, as a choice has to be made between various paths, once it is inevitable that young adult offenders will come within the criminal justice system.

At first sight the choice seemed to be limited to:

— either their inclusion - at least partly - in the system for minors;
— or their inclusion in the scope of criminal law, but with the imposition of lighter penalties;
— or the drafting of a *lex specialis* relating to them.

A very wide variety of opinions was expressed, and several participants were against the creation of a special status for young adults. They backed up their viewpoint with various arguments: it would be preferable to place more emphasis on the offence than on the person when establishing a framework for intervention, and it is more important to develop a reaction of high legal quality, not excluding adults from the search for more positive solutions for the offender and society, and emphasising the fact that the judicial reaction should highlight the damage caused, the disturbance of public order and the injured victim rather than the crime. They noted that young adults dealt with under the law relating to minors were sometimes treated more harshly than they would have been had the general criminal law been applied to them.

Others, in contrast, considered that the basis had to be the law relating to minors, which should be allowed to be applied to young adults - at least until the age of 18-21 -on the basis of Article 3 of the Beijing Rules adopted by the United Nations in November 1985. Those who held this view argued that it was important to give young adults the advantages of the juvenile justice system, thus preventing them from entering the stigmatising adult criminal law system, and to urge that this age group, in contrast, be given the education, assistance and protection available under the law relating to minors. As juvenile delinquency had been reduced through this approach, why should the system not be applied to young adults who were effectively experiencing psychological and social difficulties delaying their arrival at a social "age of majority"? Would this not be one way of preventing them from establishing a foothold on the ladder of crime ?

Yet others expressed the view that it was now important to remove any age-based distinction between offenders: all should be subject to a general criminal law. In such a scenario, the law relating to minors and special juvenile courts would have no more sense than a specific law for young adults. It is obvious that adoption of this radical view would inevitably cause an upheaval in criminology and bring about far-reaching changes of criminal law as a whole. Is this a vision of the future or a Utopia ?

The great variety of opinions on this subject voiced at the colloquium related mainly to theoretical problems. It did not hide the fact that a good number of countries, through their legislative practice, provide for account to be taken of the young adult age group, with measures ranging from inclusion in the system relating to minors to a reduction of the penalties applicable under the general criminal law, and to different ways of executing sentences. In this context, it does not really seem acceptable that certain countries still make no appropriate provision for young adults, not even in the shape of lighter penalties.

The idea of designing special legislation for young adults was not adopted, although it would have been conceivable for such new legislation, in the long term, to become the general criminal law, with heavier penalties for adults.

3.2.3 Courts with jurisdiction in juvenile matters

The idea of setting up special courts for young adult offenders was not adopted by the colloquium.

On the other hand, there was a long discussion of the benefits and drawbacks of dealing with young adults in juvenile courts. It was in fact noted that juvenile court judges are generally specialists, and that the decline in juvenile delinquency in certain countries would make it possible for them to make their competence available to young adults, without the state incurring excessive additional expenditure.

While some object to this proposal on the grounds that juvenile courts in some countries are in crisis, the reaction of others was that they did not intend to sacrifice a century of efforts to create juvenile courts because of certain perverse effects, and that, in contrast, it was important to extend their jurisdiction to young adults, at least up to the age of 21, and to take all necessary steps to mitigate the disadvantages of this system.

3.2.4 The procedural rules

The course of justice is often slow, especially where ordinary courts are concerned. It is, however, essential for young adults to benefit from a rapid procedure enabling them to grasp the link between their offence and the resulting penalty. This would tend to suggest that they should be dealt with - at least until reaching a specific age - by juvenile courts, which are supposed to act more speedily.

The *lex mitior* must be applied to young adults, so that they benefit from the more favourable treatment when the age which they reach by the time of their trial entails a change of status.

These principles were unanimously accepted, and all who spoke also emphasised the absolute need to guarantee respect for young adults' basic rights, whichever court they were to appear before.

3.2.5 The basic principles of court action

Crime trends have their own history, which cannot fail to influence the law relating to young adult offenders.

The punitive and retributory model seems, to some extent, to have given way to a social defence approach advocating individualised measures, taking account of young adults' personality with a view to treating them and mending their ways, rather than of the objective seriousness of the offence.

However, a neo-classical trend, advocating "just deserts", appeared in the United States a few years ago, and this has sometimes even been extended to minors. Could this soon influence Europe, as far as its eastern frontiers ? If so, that would be a regrettable backward step in criminological philosophy.

Stemming from the ideas of 1968, a critical tendency towards society, institutions and the law produced advocates of a broad liberal movement - known as the "three Ds": decriminalisation, depenalisation and disinstitutionalisation - for social strategies and diversion measures in the criminological sphere. These ideas - still present - have made a huge impact on western societies.

The 10th Criminological Colloquium nevertheless devoted particular attention to a new criminological trend linked to a change of mentality in many western countries: that of reparation, in the form of either diversion or penalties. Did one participant not say that, *"with this in prospect, it would no longer be a matter of meeting one wrong with another, as in the law of retaliation, but one of righting a wrong by repairing the damage and restoring the disturbed order; if this is to be done, we should adopt a more realistic approach and give up both our moralising attitude of punishing wrongs and our missionary zeal to convert all offenders !"*

By endeavouring to have the damage caused by the offence repaired, whether in reality or symbolically - if possible restoring the *status quo* - we take account of the victim's interests and too long neglected viewpoint, restore public order, which should be of concern to everyone living in a democracy, and make it possible for the perpetrator to assuage his guilt, shoulder his responsibilities and accept the consequences of his acts, making the process an educational one. These principles should be applied to offenders regardless of age, but they are obviously particularly relevant to young adults.

Still, reparatory justice cannot be regarded as a panacea ! For we are only just beginning to define the concepts of, and implement, these principles, which require a careful process of staged tests and a constant comparison of theory and practice. This is a stimulating area of research for criminologists, who are well aware that tension exists between the restorative model and the guarantees provided by the law, and that appropriate equipment must be available if such tests are to be successful.

The colloquium was alert to the ethical, psychological and social grounds for this model for young adult offenders, recommending development of a system to meet the methodological and technical needs of reparatory penalties and mediation; it hoped that diversion measures would also focus on reparation and reconciliation.

However, several participants emphasised the need to attach due weight to the seriousness of the offence committed and to the principle of proportionality, showing the young adult the relationship between his offence and the penalty imposed. In the words of one of the criminologists present: *"In general criminal law, the penalty is a response to the offence; in the law governing minors, it is above all a preventive reaction to an unfavourable social situation and to behaviour which breaks the law; the young adult, for his part, needs an equitable reaction and an acceptance of personal responsibility."*

3.2 The system of penalties

With this in mind, punitive measures such as disqualification from driving, confiscation or return of stolen goods, payment of the fine by the young person himself, etc. may be encouraged.

While deprivations of liberty are unavoidable, the colloquium - in the light of all the international meetings of the past hundred years and more - stressed the urgent need for these to take place under a special scheme and on premises not shared by adults, and even in establishments for adolescents up to the age of 21, where detainees have access to resources enabling them effectively to reintegrate into the world of work and society. Additionally, such detention should be for as brief a period as possible, as there seems to be no justification for prolonging such confinement for allegedly educational purposes.

The use of detention on remand must remain exceptional, and not mask a brief sentence of deprivation of liberty.

It is of the greatest importance that there should be a highly available health service in all establishments where young adults are detained, capable of dealing with the many physical and psychological problems associated with drug-taking, Aids, homosexuality and depression.

It is self-evident that measures such as the intensive monitoring of probation, suspended sentences and provisional releases are still very valuable. Many countries are now developing other ways of looking after young adults, examples being intensive intermediate treatment, supervision of reparation following mediation, community service orders, the monitoring of treatment for drug addicts and alcoholics, advice, training assistance and support, etc.

These measures may be implemented in the community, the young person continuing to live in his usual circle - which may play a supporting role - or in appropriate premises of various kinds, where daytime work is allowed either outside or in confinement, nights and/or weekends are spent in detention, depending on the need for staffing, etc.

To these may be added all the intermediate structures and small community facilities serving as focal points for young adults breaking away from their roots, whether or not they are offenders. These places offer or insist on an educational framework of varying degrees of strictness, and some also provide therapeutic support.

4. SOCIAL AND VOLUNTARY WORKERS

Whether it be sentences of detention, suspended sentences, probation, etc. or the various kinds of semi-liberty and the back-up for the execution of alternative penalties - the latter being preferred by participants in the colloquium - there is always a need for the efforts of competent social and/or voluntary workers.

Now that most European countries are experiencing economic problems, a realistic crime policy is needed, one which must take account of the costs and benefits of action. We all know that imprisonment, especially if it is an attempt to reintegrate young adults into the world of work and society, is very costly, while the results achieved give rise to legitimate doubts as to whether the investment is worthwhile for society and detainees.

On the other hand, there are, almost everywhere in western Europe, a host of official or private social services deploying social workers whose efficiency could be improved if their activities were better managed and co-ordinated in terms of prevention, social strategies and action ordered by courts, and if they were carefully and systematically evaluated. What wastage of energies and funds there is in this area ! What problems there are of co-operation and of wastage of time and energy because the professionals fail to co-ordinate their action with that of local authorities and volunteers !

It is high time to instil order where it is lacking. The fundamental remedy will be a change in social worker training, which needs improving in several fields, including the methods taught (less learning about the individual relationship with those requiring assistance, and more about group work and community action), motivation for dynamic action rather than a lethargic bureaucratic approach, and, above all, acceptance of work ordered by the courts, to which a good many social workers react unwillingly, for ideological and personal reasons. Suitable training ought to enable them to accept the role of communicators of the mutual needs of their clients and society, acting as a sort of effective "social indicator" giving young adults the information they need about the demands of that society and informing society of any omissions or failings in the policy pursued.

In the countries of eastern Europe, much hope is being placed in the assistance of private associations able to give great help in terms of support for young adult offenders. In the west, too, better use of voluntary services should make it possible to favour alternative penalties rather than deprivations of liberty, and to advocate a resolutely innovative crime policy towards this age group. The instruments are there, so it is just a matter of knowing how to use them judiciously by giving them the necessary motivation and back-up !

135

5.   THE ROLES OF THOSE INVOLVED IN CRIME POLICY

The conclusions and recommendations of the colloquium show new reformist tendencies. If they are to be taken up, it is important that the various parties which are going to draw on them to prepare, implement and evaluate crime policy should be persuaded of its value and willing to co-operate with interest and conviction. So all who contribute to the policy must be involved in its implementation: political authorities, policy-makers, the Public Prosecutor's Department, the police, the judiciary and the staff responsible for execution in one capacity or another. Not only must their individual awareness be aroused, but encouragement must also be given to the setting up of interdisciplinary think-tanks, where all can voice their opinions and criticism and help with the step-by-step evaluation of the work done on the ground. Researchers should not be kept apart from this gradual creation of new structures and organisations, experimental models and genuine co-operation.

When cash is short, any social or crime policy must be comprehensive, carefully targeted and consistent, avoiding duplication, gaps resulting from poor co-ordination and lack of complementarity of strategies and tactics; in this way, sceptics and opponents at every level of decision and execution will find themselves facing a solid common front.

6.   THE PUBLIC AND THE MEDIA

Crime policy is part of general national, regional and local policy. In my view, we should not say, as many readily do, that policy is "the art of the possible", but call it "the art of making what is necessary possible." In order to make people aware of this opposite angle - particularly during a period of economic problems - it is essential to make a considerable effort to provide public information.

It is not enough to show that the proposed reforms are based on values accepted in theory in the Declaration of Human Rights and applied to the treatment of young adult offenders; they must be demonstrated to be likely to improve life in society, going beyond the inevitable tension between apparently conflicting interests.

This raising of public awareness is all the more urgent for the fact that young adult crime is often regarded as a threat to public safety and order, and that an appetite for the sensational makes the media exaggerate the "dangerous" nature of young adult offenders. So criminologists have a duty to patiently shape public opinion, preventing

feelings of fear, explaining the crime policy reforms adopted, making the consequences, costs and benefits of these options clear and winning the support and co-operation of local communities, and untying the purse strings of thestate and the private associations concerned.

Obviously the provision of information to the public requires the help of the media, which must be won over to the new ideas and planned reforms, such as community service orders and mediation either within the community or by a professional mediator.

This patient provision of information is crucial to what can be achieved in terms of a reform of crime policy *vis-à-vis* young adults. Why not make use of some of the marketing methods used by firms in order to promote innovative ideas in this area ? It is no longer a question of good works and paternalistic charity, but of well designed and managed programmes to be placed before the public.

7.   RESEARCH

Research is essential to give credibility to this policy on young adult crime, not only to extend criminologists' scientific knowledge, but also to give the reforms a basis of reliable facts that can be put before policy-makers and public.

In "Greater Europe" it is vital - as participants in the 10th Criminological Colloquium emphasised - for studies to be conducted in all countries, giving a clearer view on a comparative basis of young adult crime; now that delinquency is crossing frontiers with alarming speed, this is a matter of urgency. These studies must, *inter alia*, enable age group research covering Europe to be carried out and make it possible to examine the types and origins of offences, repeated offences and the impact on the environment of this delinquency. Only afterwards will it be possible to draw up social and crime policies appropriate to that environment.

Several speakers also stressed the importance of knowing more about young adults' own thoughts and how they would wish to be treated as either perpetrators or victims of crime. Information about this is very incomplete or non-existent, but more would provide valuable indications for the development of an appropriate and effective crime policy. If we ask their opinion we show a kind of respect towards them !

The prime aim for each country will be, taking existing structures as the starting point, to survey current equipment and develop it cleverly and imaginatively, after studying actual needs.

Qualitative research must be conducted alongside the statistical and quantitative studies, so that we can refine the perception of crime and that of the effects of the crime policy adopted.

It is not enough to determine the extent of young adult crime. It is important to develop research with a view to evaluation in all the areas concerned: the effectiveness of the various strategies for action, costs and benefits, diversion measures, as well as experimental research into the new alternative penalties, and more particularly the effects of community service orders and the various forms of mediation. It is only studies of this kind that will enable application to be improved and effectiveness to be measured, all aspects which, far from being of interest only to criminologists, will also have an impact on those responsible for formulating crime policy and the public.

CONCLUSION

If we had to find a way to describe this 10th Criminological Colloquium, we could say that, in many respects, it was a rich adventure off the beaten track: as insufficient work had been done previously to investigate the subject of young adult crime, the ideas discussed were often original, and the presence of representatives from eastern Europe proved highly stimulating.

It has been made clear that today's young adults face serious difficulties and very much need to be regarded as fully-fledged, respected and valued human beings. Realisation of their vulnerability has led to the emergence of some innovative ideas, which may subsequently extend to both minors and adults, guiding penology, criminology and social action through uncharted waters.

None of us were unaware of the changes being experienced in European society and the range of problems to be tackled; this Europe, through its diversity, must achieve unity of spirit while respecting each country's historical and cultural context. Some challenge!

Each country is aware of the dangers ahead of it as it draws up a policy on young adult offenders. In the east, there is the temptation to destroy the past heritage, instead of saving the good features, and the attraction of a return to neo-classical theories. For the west, there is the risk of the reappearance of these theories and the inconsistencies of disordered and poorly targeted social and crime policies which have so little credibility that public opinion is against them.

All criminologists need a vision, a shared intuition, as well as their scientific knowledge; it is an act of courage. As J. Derrida, the philosopher, wrote, *"Every time there is responsibility to be taken, a sort of experience of the impossible has to be lived through."* This experience of the impossible, which we are asking young adults to go through, is something that we, too, must face.

CONCLUSIONS AND RECOMMENDATIONS

by
Mrs V. Lenoir-Degoumois
General Rapporteur, Professor Emeritus,
University of Lausanne (Switzerland)

Young adults differ from both adolescents and adults by dint of special features of a psychological, social and criminological kind.

The build-up of their social and personal identity sometimes remains uncertain. Their position in society is not yet clear and their aspirations may be at odds with what their surroundings offer. The ambivalence of this situation can cause frustration and rebellion, in turn leading to various forms of deviance or delinquency.

Criminality among young adults focuses mainly on crimes against property. It occupies a relatively large place in registered general crime. Frequently associated with a degree of marginalisation, it may express itself in high-risk, and even suicidal, behaviour such as drug addiction, hooliganism at sports events, aggressive conduct on the roads and aggression against minorities. Criminality among young adults tends to diminish with age, permitting a favourable prognosis in many cases.

The social policy of prevention and the strategies have to be adapted to the specific needs of young adults. Although in this context the provisions of Council of Europe Recommendation No. R (87) 20 on social reactions to juvenile delinquency and the conclusions of the 19th Criminological Research Conference are still highly relevant, stress should none the less be laid on the effective vocational integration of young adults and on the creation of openings suited to their abilities, so as to enable them to achieve a measure of independence and cope with their financial problems, if any. They should be provided with more points of support within the local community.

Greater attention should also be paid to developing every possible technical method of dissuasion.

Among the social strategies for preventing young adults from becoming involved in the criminal justice system, emphasis should be laid in particular on methods of diversion based on reparation and on reconciliation.

A wide range of opinions was expressed in regard to the status to be accorded to young adults when their involvement in the criminal justice system can no longer be avoided. However, it is observed that most countries make legislative provision for special arrangements for young adults; these range from various ways of executing sanctions to placement on an equal footing with minors, and may include mitigation of sentence.

On the other hand, the colloquium was not in favour of special courts being set up for young adults. It weighed up the advantages and drawbacks of extending the regime applicable to minors to young adults; such an extension could only be contemplated provided there were similar procedural guarantees to those under the adult criminal law and should take account of the risk of adverse discriminatory effects.

Recommendations

Regardless of the system chosen, and since there was unanimity on a number of points, the colloquium agreed on the following principles:

\ — effective social policies should be developed in order to improve young people's welfare and promote their integration into the working world;

— young adults should receive a guarantee that their fundamental rights will be respected, both as regards procedural rules and enforcement of penalties;

— due weight should be given to the nature and seriousness of the offence committed through stricter application of the principle of proportionality, also taking into account the personality of the offender;

— detention on remand should be avoided wherever possible, being all too often used as a disguised form of short-term penalty;

— deprivation of liberty should be replaced wherever possible by alternative sanctions of a varied and constructive kind;

— where deprivation of liberty, for the shortest possible time, proves unavoidable, it should be handled in such a way as to allow for the social reintegration of the young person and be carried out in a specific place;

— techniques should be developed which fulfil the methodological and technical requirements of penalties involving reparation and mediation;

— resources already available should be better managed and evaluated and adapted to work with young adults.

The colloquium also considers it desirable that :

— the public should be informed about the delinquency of young adults and about the crime policy and social policy pursued to deal with it;

— those states which have not yet done so should incorporate in the legislation applicable to young adults such alternative sanctions as mediation, community service and intermediate treatment;

— states with penal legislation specific to minors should consider the feasibility of extending its scope to cover young adults below the age of 21;

— those states which cannot contemplate extending the scope of the juvenile criminal law should adapt the general legislation to take account of the specific needs of young adult offenders;

— states should ensure that criminal proceedings are speedy in the case of young adults and that the more lenient regime is applied to them if their age has led to a change of status by the time judgment is delivered;

— the authorities concerned should redefine and give new impetus to the judicial professions (judges, police, etc.) and the social work professions, enabling them to work as effectively as possible with young adults, and should promote interdisciplinary training;

— states should facilitate the work of voluntary organisations involved in crime policy towards young adults;

— the scientific community should devise joint instruments in order to conduct comparative research into criminality among young adults and to promote evaluation studies of the relevant crime policies;

— the Council of Europe should follow up the colloquium by continuing to work on the matching of social and criminal law responses to crime among young adults;

— the Council of Europe should arrange at the earliest opportunity for publication of the colloquium proceedings and their widest possible distribution among those responsible for working out and implementing crime policy.

Sales agents for publications of the Council of Europe
Agents de vente des publications du Conseil de l'Europe

AUSTRALIA/AUSTRALIE
Hunter Publications, 58A, Gipps Street
AUS-3066 COLLINGWOOD, Victoria

AUSTRIA/AUTRICHE
Gerold und Co., Graben 31
A-1011 WIEN 1

BELGIUM/BELGIQUE
La Librairie européenne SA
50, avenue A. Jonnart
B-1200 BRUXELLES 20

Jean de Lannoy
202, avenue du Roi
B-1060 BRUXELLES

CANADA
Renouf Publishing Company Limited
1294 Algoma Road
CDN-OTTAWA ONT K1B 3W8

CYPRUS/CHYPRE
MAM
The House of the Cyprus Book
PO Box 1722, CY-NICOSIA

DENMARK/DANEMARK
Munksgaard
Book and Subscription Service
PO Box 2148
DK-1016 KØBENHAVN K

FINLAND/FINLANDE
Akateeminen Kirjakauppa
Keskuskatu 1, PO Box 218
SF-00381 HELSINKI

GERMANY/ALLEMAGNE
UNO Verlag
Poppelsdorfer Allee 55
D-53115 BONN

GREECE/GRÈCE
Librairie Kauffmann
Mavrokordatou 9, GR-ATHINAI 106 78

IRELAND/IRLANDE
Government Stationery Office
Publications Section
Bishop Street, IRL-DUBLIN 8

ISRAEL/ISRAËL
ROY International
PO Box 13056
IL-61130 TEL AVIV

ITALY/ITALIE
Libreria Commissionaria Sansoni
Via Duca di Calabria, 1/1
Casella Postale 552, I-50125 FIRENZE

LUXEMBOURG
Librairie Bourbon
(Imprimerie Saint-Paul)
11, rue Bourbon
L-1249 LUXEMBOURG

NETHERLANDS/PAYS-BAS
InOr-publikaties, PO Box 202
NL-7480 AE HAAKSBERGEN

NORWAY/NORVÈGE
Akademika, A/S Universitetsbokhandel
PO Box 84, Blindern
N-0314 OSLO

PORTUGAL
Livraria Portugal, Rua do Carmo, 70
P-1200 LISBOA

SPAIN/ ESPAGNE
Mundi-Prensa Libros SA
Castelló 37, E-28001 MADRID

Llibreria de la Generalitat
Rambla dels Estudis, 118
E-08002 BARCELONA

Llibreria de la Generalitat de Catalunya
Gran Via Jaume I, 38, E-17001 GIRONA

SWEDEN/SUÈDE
Aktiebolaget CE Fritzes
Regeringsgatan 12, Box 163 56
S-10327 STOCKHOLM

SWITZERLAND/SUISSE
Buchhandlung Heinimann & Co.
Kirchgasse 17, CH-8001 ZÜRICH

BERSY
Route du Manège 60
CP 4040
CH-1950 SION 4

TURKEY/TURQUIE
Yab-Yay Yayimcilik Sanayi Dagitim Tic Ltd
Barbaros Bulvari 61 Kat 3 Daire 3
Besiktas, TR-ISTANBUL

UNITED KINGDOM/ROYAUME-UNI
HMSO, Agency Section
51 Nine Elms Lane
GB-LONDON SW8 5DR

UNITED STATES and CANADA/
ÉTATS-UNIS et CANADA
Manhattan Publishing Company
1 Croton Point Avenue, PO Box 650
CROTON, NY 10520

STRASBOURG
Librairie internationale Kléber
1, rue des Francs-Bourgeois
F-67000 STRASBOURG

Librairie des Facultés
2-12, rue de Rome
F-67000 STRASBOURG

Librairie Kléber
Palais de l'Europe
F-67075 STRASBOURG Cedex

Council of Europe Press/Les éditions du Conseil de l'Europe
Council of Europe/Conseil de l'Europe
F-67075 Strasbourg Cedex